T0364141

Procurement 4.0

h&z is an employee-owned management consultancy founded in 1997 by Rainer Hoffmann and Dr. Thomas Zachau. Today h&z has over 300 professionals in all major markets and is among the leading consultancies for procurement and supply chain management. From SMEs to global players – more than 500 companies trust h&z to boost their procurement function to serve as a strategic success factor in global competition. Following the philosophy of »Consulting with Head, Heart, and Hand«, h&z works closely with its clients to create maximum impact. h&z combines thought leadership with an understanding of the client's particular corporate culture. This enables h&z to master the transition from great concepts to operational implementation success.

Dr. Alexander Batran, Agnes Erben, Ralf Schulz, Franziska Sperl

Procurement 4.0

A survival guide in a digital, disruptive world

Campus Verlag
Frankfurt/New York

ISBN 978-3-593-50669-2 Print
ISBN 978-3-593-43566-4 E-Book (PDF)

Cover design: Guido Klütsch, Köln
Cover illustration: Getty Images/fStop
Typesetting: Fotosatz L. Huhn, Linsengericht
Printing: Beltz Bad Langensalza
Printed in Germany

www.campus.de

CONTENTS

Overview of interviews 7

Preface 9

A letter from Procurement Leaders by David Rae 11

The survivalists guide to Procurement 4.0 15

Discover your blind spot beyond tier 1 25

Stop groping in the dark for innovation 45

Solving the 4.0 leadership challenge 99

The truth lies in the cloud 121

Push the button 165

Abbreviations 167

About the authors 169

Notes 171

Index 173

OVERVIEW OF INTERVIEWS

Discover your blind spot beyond tier 1

»Digitization comes second – process design comes first«
Matthias Krause-Uhrmann, Director, CPO, BP Europe SE

»Typical Apple users have to feel comfortable with procurement tools«
Andreas Abrath, Director, Project Head »Complexity Reduction in Procurement«, BASF

Stop groping in the dark for innovation

»Supplier satisfaction is the key to improved supplier interaction«
Prof. Holger Schiele, Technology Management – Innovation of Operations, University of Twente

»We will raise the relationships with our suppliers to the next level«
Dr. Thomas Papke, VP Corporate Sourcing, Lufthansa

»We're going to the edge – to get our digital strategy ready by the end of the year«
Jochen Weyandt, EVP, Head of Group Business Services & CPO, OC Oerlikon Corporation AG

»We got the wake-up call some time ago«
Martin Austermann, Senior Vice President Group Sourcing, Husqvarna Group

Solving the 4.0 leadership challenge

»Procurement is about to reach new heights as an end-to-end solutions provider«
Dr. Michael Nießen, CPO, Deutsche Post DHL

»From good to great – we supply for success«
Dr. Johann Wieland, Former Head of Indirect Purchasing, BMW Group, now CEO of BMW Group and Brilliance Automotive (China) Holding

»Unleash the power of data«
Dr. Armin Beckert, VP, Head of Supply Chain Strategy & Business Support, Airbus Defence v& Space

The truth lies in the cloud

»Speed is the real deal«
Claus Hahne, VP Corporate Procurement, ProSiebenSat.1 Media AG

»Digitization of procurement is spot on what we are doing«
Jacob Gorm Larsen, Director of Digital Procurement, Maersk

»Time is money – we need to accelerate the speed of procurement processes«
Dr. Turan Sahin, CPO, Allianz Managed Operations & Services SE

PREFACE

Procurement is without a doubt at an important turning point and might have to redefine itself in terms of its role as a business function or even regarding its reason for being. In such uncertain and fuzzy times, it can be helpful to stop for a moment and freeze the status quo.

At this special moment in time, we from h&z decided to write a book on »Procurement 4.0«, addressing the huge challenges procurement will have to face. There will not be fewer tasks, but definitely different ones in terms of what we buy and how we buy.

With this book, we dare to take a glimpse into the future while broadening the overall picture: »Digital« is only a small aspect of Procurement 4.0, even more challenges lie, for example, in the organizations we need to design for tomorrow or the people we need to choose, leveraging the supply base while creating winning value chains.

And, as one CPO put it recently: »We want Procurement 4.0, but we have Staff 2.0 and even Leadership 1.0.«

Fortunately, we didn't have to go all the way on our own. We'd like to thank the contributors from leading industrial corporations for sharing their opinions and insights in the form of interviews and use cases.

Stefan Aichbauer
Managing Partner at h&z

A LETTER FROM PROCUREMENT LEADERS BY DAVID RAE

Challenges ahead – an outlook by Procurement Leaders

There has been a great deal of debate over recent years about how the ongoing march of technology might undermine our way of life; with robots stealing our jobs, computers driving our cars and artificial intelligence (AI) systems surpassing human intelligence on their way to taking over the world.

While much of this debate is fueled by headline-loving journalists' and entrepreneurs' intent on creating a feeding frenzy around a particular trend or technology, the fact remains that we are living through an intense and unprecedented period of change. Not only is technology advancing at an astonishing rate, when coupled with other trends such as population growth, rapid urbanization, climate change and an intense and increasing energy dependency, we face some interesting challenges ahead.

The advances made in technology, of course, are in many cases a commercial reaction to the challenges we face as a society. Tesla CEO Elon Musk's vision and determination to disrupt both the energy and automotive sectors are a good example; but so are the advances made in the pharmaceutical and healthcare sectors on disease control and the focus on genetically-enhanced farming methods. All direct responses to current and emerging global trends.

The point here is that the commercial sector is as responsible for solving our future challenges as our governments. We are living through a period of social entrepreneurialism; where, for many, a desire to make money is matched by a desire to solve the most pressing issues we face as a society.

So, why is this important to procurement?

The reality is that the pace of change and scale of challenge that we are faced with demand a new approach to how we do business. Call it what you will; but in simple terms it demands gaining a greater understanding of our world through advanced data analytics, being quick to react to situations as they arise and being more open to collaboration with third parties to help solve those challenges. In each of these areas, digital technologies are a key enabler and in each of these areas, CPOs must assess their own capabilities and approaches and determine how they can support and contribute to the overall strategy.

Knowledge is power

There are many examples of how procurement can make better use of data, both in the traditional sense through improved spend and category analysis; but also in new and emerging areas such as advanced data analytics and the Internet of Things (IoT).

Advanced data analytics can be used to provide more visibility to the business for planning and forecasting purposes, using real-time data such as commodity and labor prices to help predict individual-product production costs on an ongoing basis. In theory, this can help companies work to rolling forecasts and mean procurement can be much closer aligned with, and supporting of, sales and marketing tactics.

Meanwhile, the impact of IoT continues to be felt, with the supply chain a key playground – visibility of individual goods and components in the supply chain can be greatly improved, with a subsequent improvement in efficiency, which in many cases can lead to a significant cash benefit. At the recent Procurement Leaders World Procurement Congress, Flextronics' CPO Tom Linton provided a good example, explaining how taking five days out of his 65-day supply chain through enhanced visibility provided $350 million in cash to the business.

Speed is of the essence

The same thinking can be extended to agility and the benefits that come from being able to react to market conditions and opportunities. Being able to easily ramp up or slow down production to take advantage of peaks and troughs in consumer demand without holding large quantities of inventory is a growing differentiator in corporate performance and, ultimately, shareholder return.

Being able to react quickly to global events – whether positive or negative – is another key differentiator, and something CPOs can look to digital technologies for to help solve. For example, digital dashboards that offer a real-time view of a supply chain and suppliers, and how wider political and economic issues are affecting them, can help drive faster, more effective decisions.

However, perhaps the largest, or, at least, most widely experienced, impact of digital technology over the past 20 years, is in the world of communication. Thanks to this technology, we are permanently connected with and have immediate visibility into the activities of billions of individuals all across the world, which brings with it fundamental opportunities.

Entire business models have naturally been built on these opportunities, but for traditional businesses, and therefore the procurement functions that serve them, the impact of this revolution is more subtle.

The end of not invented here

Although individuals are now accustomed to sharing and being open with the entire planet, the corporate world is slower to adapt. But adapt it has to, and one of the ways in which procurement has a major role to play comes with the breaking down of traditional corporate boundaries.

Chrysler's Extended Enterprise model and its famous Supplier Cost Reduction Effort (Score) from the 1990s are both well-known approaches to supply management that have been the subject of many articles and academic theses.

But while predominantly focused on cost control, companies today are looking to break down corporate barriers to access new technologies, new solutions and new product developments. This is different and new, and procurement has the opportunity to manage and facilitate the process with suppliers, and potentially other third parties.

Because procurement sits in the privileged position of having visibility of relationships with thousands of suppliers, as well as connections with the entire business, we are perfectly placed to manage the processes that enable advanced collaboration between otherwise autonomous organizations.

We can increasingly rely on technology to manage much of the procurement process, freeing up time and resources to spend on more strategic and value-adding activities. Rather than having a conversation with suppliers on price, or even total cost, procurement should be facilitating a wider discussion around opportunity and capability. Rather than viewing third-party spend as a cost that needs to be reduced, we should be looking at it as an investment that demands a return.

At Procurement Leaders, we call this new focus supplier-enabled innovation (SEI), and at its core it means handing your company the keys to the expertise, collective brainpower and R&D budgets of the supply base. Of course, it isn't one-way traffic – for true SEI to take place, suppliers must benefit significantly and fairly from the collaboration in order for the partnership to be effective. Neither is this a short-term win; companies must invest for the long term in SEI and supplier partnerships in order to see a return.

But if you were to ask me what the biggest impact is that CPOs can make to their organizations over the next 20 years, my answer would be straightforward – to provide the means by which their companies can work with leading suppliers collaboratively and benefit from their expertise, capabilities and solutions.

Digital technologies will be a key enabler for this shift – and it's a shift that will allow procurement to facilitate the collaboration required to solve some of the biggest problems our societies have yet faced.

David Rae
Content & Community Director at Procurement Leaders

THE SURVIVALISTS GUIDE TO PROCUREMENT 4.0

Industry 4.0, or the fourth industrial revolution, is well underway. There is a lot of talk surrounding this latest industrial trend where digital technologies, including cyber-physical systems, the Internet of Things, cloud robotics, 3D printing, sensor technology and big data, are dominating the agenda and reshaping industry and the way we work. A search on Google for »Industry 4.0« will reveal about 116 million sources, so there is clearly a strong community building up around this topic, offering ideas, insights and support.

What has happened so far

It all started out with the invention of the steam engine, which was the birth of industrialization and which enabled the shift from an agricultural to an industrial economy. In the mid–19th century, the second industrial revolution was enabled by inventions like the combustion engine and assembly line, boosted also by electricity. As automation proceeded and computers offered completely new possibilities, the next industrial age was heralded. Today we are on the move into the so-called fourth industrial revolution, where more and more tasks will be executed by machines or artificial intelligence, which brings us back to the above-mentioned cyber-physical systems, i.e. connected machines.

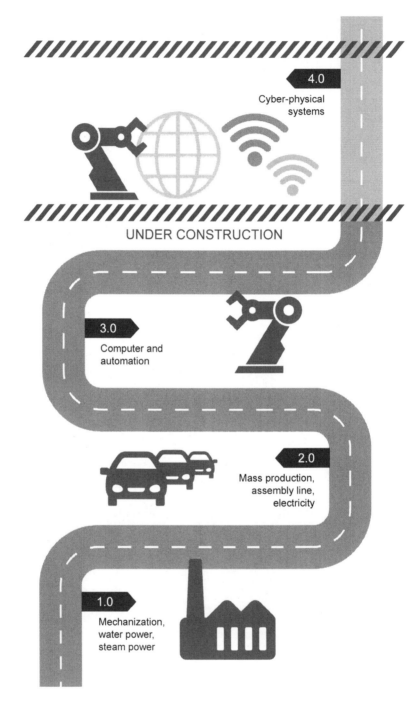

4.0
Cyber-physical systems

UNDER CONSTRUCTION

3.0
Computer and automation

2.0
Mass production, assembly line, electricity

1.0
Mechanization, water power, steam power

Phases of industrial revolutions

And what about Procurement 4.0?

Try a Google search again, now for Procurement 4.0 and there are comparatively few hits, just over 12 million in fact – and even fewer for the global term of »procurement digitization«. When you consider that procurement is the function that manages the 70–80 % of the external value add that most companies are looking for, this imbalance seems very disproportionate. It appears that procurement's role in Industry 4.0 is being overshadowed and that the focus is on other business functions that will be affected by this new industrial revolution. What does this suggest about the future of procurement?

Procurement will not be devoured by these digital technologies. On the contrary, as the business function with the most internal and external interfaces within the value chain, those who work in procurement will be confronted with new challenges and opportunities.

Are you ready for this new Procurement 4.0 environment?

Strip everything else away and it can be seen that at the very heart of Procurement 4.0 are questions about changes in what to buy and how to buy.

What to buy

Digitization enables new business models and therefore new product markets and categories. Customization beats standard product lines and generally there is a shift from plain products and services to whole ecosystems. The speed of innovation and time-to-market are accelerating. All industries and business models are affected by disruptive technologies. Simply the question how fast it will happen and how big the impact will be.

The automotive industry has been deeply affected by digitization and is a high-profile example that illustrates to what extent the scope of »what to buy« has changed. After 100 years of optimizing mechanically-oriented driving performance, the automotive industry is now focusing its considerable power on connectivity, electric motors and fully autonomous, self-driving vehicles. This has changed almost everything on the supply side. Huge players like Google and Apple are now suppliers to the automotive industry. The nature of supply-critical categories has changed, as illustrated by the consortium of BMW, Daimler and VW (Audi) that bought HERE, a company for digital mapping. And because a car is no longer a car but a fully connected mobility solution, new categories like apps and software for autonomous driving are firmly on the automotive buyer's radar.

How to buy

Disruptive key technologies most often come from suppliers that require intelligent approaches to safeguard their own competitiveness by differentiating themselves from the competition. How that can be solved in a situation where an OEM works together with the same 1st tier suppliers is hard to answer in just one sentence. How do you identify and get in touch with innovative suppliers, establish an exclusive relationship and keep them away from your competitors? That's not an easy task. Internal and external collaboration models will have to be redefined.

On the other hand, opportunities born out of technology and market offerings for procurement systems and apps have never been better. Cloud technology has significantly reduced entry barriers for new market players, so there are more than 100 apps for Rfx out there and ready to be put to use. It's up to procurement professionals to harvest and leverage the opportunities to improve future competitiveness. New applications are being developed at breakneck speed and some early adopters are already using them. Nobody wants to talk about the »app-ification« of the system landscape and business processes yet, but the vision for this has been clearly outlined.

What does top management across the world think of Procurement 4.0?

A CPO's snapshot of »Procurement 4.0« in 2016

Obviously, Procurement 4.0 is in its infancy and the picture of the future is still blurry and uncertain. Speed will indeed be one of the decisive forces; so according to the maturity level of your procurement organization and other influencing factors, you might have to leapfrog one step

Word cloud from h&z Procurement 4.0 roundtable

or another to reach the top. Well-matured B2C apps, with their superior usability and better user experience design, are the benchmark for already available B2B apps which, however, are not broadly applied yet. In the B2C world, »Amazonization« has become the latest buzzword to describe customer-centric business, where the driving force is the desire to provide an increasingly excellent customer experience. Undoubtedly IT will be a building block for the future of procurement, but digitization should not be viewed as an enabler but as a driver of the changing environment. Procurement has to use digital technology to get better at what it does.

However, Procurement 4.0 must not be reduced to digitization. IT systems alone won't drive your company's competitiveness in the future.

Our point of view

»What to buy« and »How to buy« is changing. At h&z, we experienced these dimensions as a powerful and at the same time simple structure to discuss current and future challenges with procurement professionals. But final answers are still missing.

With Fukushima in 2011 and Volkswagen supplier struggles in 2016, the managing of value chains beyond tier 1 flushed onto the agenda of procurement. It's about designing competitive and reliable supplier networks or, in other words, value chains.

Disruptive technologies and shorter life cycles of products pose a severe challenge to many companies to staying competitive. It's about getting technology from the outside in, especially if intellectual property (IP) is with suppliers or internal know-how is limited to mechanical engineering. Additionally, many business models are undergoing dramatic changes from products, services and ecosystems to performance-oriented contracting and pay-per-use models. Are you ready to serve such »back-to-back models« from end customers to the supply base?

Let's pause for a moment and try to tie up some loose ends. Even if digital is the hype, Procurement 4.0 needs to be approached holistically.

- *»What to buy …«*
  … within the value chain of a network itself
  … among buyer-supplier relationships to harness internal know-how and the know-how of selected suppliers with the power of co-creation

- *»How to buy …«*
  … in agile networks by setting up a future-oriented organization, new roles, a digitally powered working model and a leadership approach
  … in an environment of increased (data) connectivity, process efficiency and collaboration by digital gadgets and a future-ready IT architecture

Have you ever thought about solutions in these four dimensions? We have – and put them together in the h&z Procurement 4.0 framework.

Competition creating competing value chains: Buyers are increasingly assuming the role of a value chain manager with a holistic view of the supply chain. This is because the design of the total supplier structure beyond tier 1 is crucial to the success and competitiveness of companies. This value chain determines the competitiveness of companies with competitors and their suppliers.

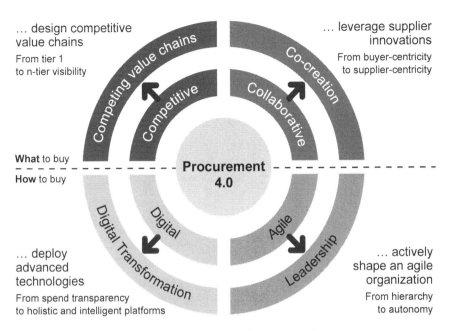

... design competitive value chains
From tier 1 to n-tier visibility

... leverage supplier innovations
From buyer-centricity to supplier-centricity

What to buy
How to buy

Procurement 4.0

... deploy advanced technologies
From spend transparency to holistic and intelligent platforms

... actively shape an agile organization
From hierarchy to autonomy

h&z Procurement 4.0 framework

Co-creation leveraging supplier innovations: Innovations are important in order to achieve differentiation. Procurement plays the lead role in identifying innovative suppliers and integrating them into the company's product development process and lifting them up to a co-creational setting. The aim of strategic networking is to be the preferred customer and, as the favorite customer, to have exclusive rights to supplier innovations.

Leadership in an agile organization: 4.0 even requires new leadership models. Time-to-market innovation and localization needs are turning organizations into an agile working environment. Functions are dissolving towards swarm organizations.

Technology deploying advanced opportunities: The technical possibilities of data analytics, especially big data and the Internet of Things, go far beyond data introduced by e-catalog, eRfx or e-auctions.

This vital period of development for purchasing to take us into Procurement 4.0 is one of the key managerial tasks for CPOs. If procurement is not to miss the boat, it now has to take its first steps.

How we structured this book

We aimed to combine theory with as much practical input as possible. Each chapter is structured in a similar way, consisting of a brief review of the status quo, current trends on the respective topic, building blocks (i.e. what are the main aspects of the topic that need to be addressed), future scenarios and a summary of the crucial points for a quick start initiative. In addition, we individually enriched the chapters with case studies, examples and interviews.

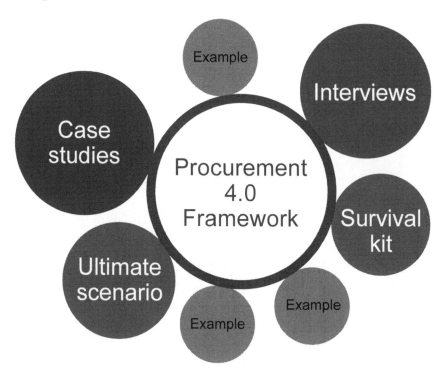

To ensure easy reading, we added some icons for you:

The *tracker* will tell you to what part of the Procurement 4.0 framework the chapters belong to,

the *magnifying glass* marks industry insights …

… and the *dialog symbol* flags interviews that we conducted with industry experts as well as academics.

Each chapter closes with a brief glance into the crystal ball and an »emergency plan«:
The section »*Think big: The ultimate scenario*« outlines the vision for professional procurement on the respective topic.

Finally, the *survival kit* provides you with a checklist of the most important points in order for you being able to kick-start actions on transforming your procurement organization towards 4.0.

DISCOVER YOUR BLIND SPOT BEYOND TIER 1

The metamorphosis from purchaser to designer

There is a generally accepted axiom in business that companies don't compete, it is value chains that compete. In fact, some would argue that the traditional model of individual businesses competing as solely autonomous entities gave way some time ago to the new model of competing value chains. It is of course based on the idea that a chain is only as strong as its weakest link, or thinking about it another way, everyone in the value chain needs to compete »as one« to gain maximum benefits for all. In some industries, digitization of products tremendously extends value chains.

Forward thinking companies that have already adopted this contemporary business model have done so because they see that value-chain-minded procurement functions can lead to substantial competitive advantage and business growth. Perspectives have changed tremendously from the days of cost cutting to looking at how suppliers can contribute to a company's product differentiation. As a result, insourcing key technologies has experienced a comeback at the expense of outsourcing.

Procurement has traditionally looked no further than its tier 1 suppliers to reap advantages but we now see, in the context of competing value chains, that this approach is too limiting. Procurement professionals need to look beyond tier 1 for the advantages they are seeking and, in fact, their role needs to change to one of value chain designers. It is this metamorphosis, from purchaser to designer, which we need to focus on in the future of procurement.

This focus on value chains, however, is not limited to the direction of tier structures up the road of one's own value chain. Procurement needs to seriously consider the customer market – its own company's product portfolio and service offerings as well as its competitors in the market. Within industries, your competitors are buying from the same suppliers – it is crucial to successfully compete to be first in getting innovations exclusively within the industry – even more as the contribution of innovations is significantly driven through the supply base with an average of more than 70% of value add from external value creation.

Extend your scope of thinking and acting

All in all, procurement should leave off concentrating on its tier 1 supply base and widen its perspective to include n-tier:

1. *Broader view:* Procurement's self-concept needs to change from driving profitability through cost optimization to additionally driving growth through differentiation – and by that evolving into a core »business« function

2. *Deeper view:* Procurement will have to understand and steer the tier structure of the supply base to create robust supply chains and best prices in sweet spots – both to reduce risk and optimize cost

3. *Outside view:* Procurement must screen and understand what the competitors in the market are doing to support and contribute to differentiation and to boost first mover advantages and exclusiveness for innovations

One might ask the question of how all of this is linked to a Procurement 4.0 discussion. In fact, digitization will change business models of industries as well as functional processes and capabilities. With new means of analytics, with new potential to create machine-to-machine communication and with further enhanced computer processing power, procurement will not only be able to extend the range of thinking and acting theoretically, but also to make it really happen. First applications can be seen in market, especially when it comes to leveraging »hidden« information from already existing data – the tipping point for achieving mass application has not been reached, but according to the insights of many of our interviewees, it will only be a matter of time.

Being cost competitive is not enough

From its origins as a cost-cutting function, procurement now plays a key role in a company's success story. Procurement's »savings hunters« are still present in some companies, while others adopt the buzzwords of »value contribution« as their guiding light. Ask any CEO and the message will be clear: Business growth and competitiveness are the main targets. If not procurement, who should ask about cost? Of course, competitive prices still do and always will contribute significantly to competitive advantages in a price-oriented environment. Nevertheless, even in B2C markets, customers are not just looking for cheap prices, they're looking for something else that distinguishes a particular product from other similar products. Porter's 1985 theory of competitive advantage states that competitiveness results not solely from cost leadership but also from product differentiation. Since outsourcing quotas throughout the industry are very high, suppliers, and the potential differentiation they can offer, have become determining factors in the race towards competitiveness and business growth.

Did you know? ...

- ... 70% of CPOs report to CFO
- ... 10% of CPOs report to COO
- ... 10% of CPOs report to CEO or are themselves a board member
- ... 10% of CPOs report to CTO, CIO

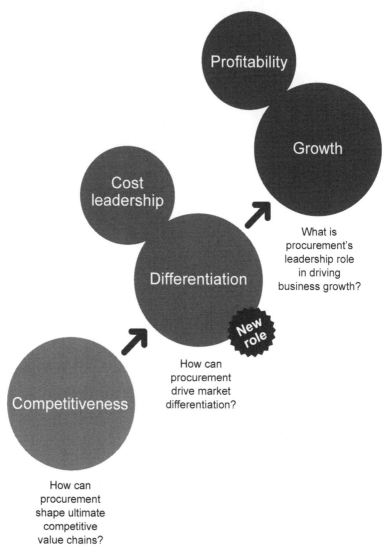

Differentiation as new role of procurement

 Example: 1960s landline phone versus 2015 smartphone

1960s landline phone: Life for buyers in the telecommunications sector was quite simple 50 years ago. The half dozen or so OEMs that produced telephones offered their customers only one standardized device in just one shade of gray. Their customers weren't offered any other choices. It took approximately 10 years before any form of product differentiation became available: The colors orange or green were offered. From a modern perspective, it is hard to believe such a product life cycle ever existed especially as the technology itself was quite simple and involved sourcing some plastic, metal and electronic parts.

2015 smartphone: There are an estimated 100+ manufacturers of smartphones, including brands and OEMs. It is difficult to know how many different devices are available these days. No one seems to have full market transparency. Today's buyers are confronted with more than 50 different suppliers per smartphone and, not surprisingly, the margins of some brands are already so low that a cost-cutting approach to procurement is redundant. Differentiation is the name of the game: Who offers the best display, or best camera, or best software, or best whatever! That's the discussion that end customers and industry journalists are having. All of these parts come from external suppliers. Buyers are asked to not only know about the latest technologies, but also to have an eye on upcoming trends, have exclusive access to key technology suppliers, know the best hardware and software suppliers, and all this in the face of shorter life cycles and a huge variety of devices. Bring back the 1960s!

You're no longer a buyer; you're a value chain thinker

To cope with the high-level requirements created by the need for differentiation, buyers in the past were asked to match their company's demand with the best-performing tier 1 direct suppliers. Again, in the 2000s, discussions around supply chain management focused on managed process links (tier 1 suppliers), monitored process links (tier 2 to possibly tier n) and non-managed process links. But recent incidents demonstrated in the harshest way that worst-case scenarios can happen. The tsunami that devastated large parts of Asia and the meltdown at the Fukushima nuclear power plant in Japan provided a shocking wake-up call about how far some procurement functions are away from value chain thinking. In the immediate aftermath of these disasters critical electronic parts from tier 2, 3 and beyond suppliers became unavailable, resulting in severe supply security issues and a shortage of supply.

Don't panic!

There was panic in procurement circles about how to solve these issues but it prompted those of us in industry to start thinking about our value chain strategies and the question, »Which suppliers should be actively monitored beyond tier one?« This went beyond mere emergency hype. It demonstrated, in the clearest possible ways, that value chain thinking is the key component to procurement's future business function. This is a positive outcome, the calm after the storm, but value chain thinking is not widespread throughout the industry. In fact, a recent h&z survey revealed that just 40% of buyers have adopted value chain thinking in their daily work.

The tactical skills of Rfx and negotiation still form the core competencies needed to effectively operate in procurement as a buyer, but following a clear business target, procurement professionals need to broaden their horizons by including value chain thinking as part of their skills portfolio.

The phone example illustrates today's challenges in a simple and clear way. Getting the best display or camera is not just a matter of knowing the suppliers. It's also about getting exclusive access. In many cases where strong suppliers are involved, such as in the automotive sector, exclusive access is hardly ever an option for a buyer. In other cases, key technologies, or key suppliers, are on a company's »make« strategy, resulting in M&A activities. This often goes beyond the idea of supply security to suit demand and can be more a matter of protectionism, keeping the technology out of reach of the competition to limit their differentiation opportunities.

There's a new buzzword in town: N-tier management

Buyers need to quickly wake up to the idea that their role has changed, that they are now value chain designers. It is frequently the case that suppliers that offer the opportunity for differentiation can't be identified and contracted at tier 1 level. This is the origin of the new trend and buzzword in procurement, n-tier management.

Ultimate competitive value chains

Now that we know what must be done, the obvious question is how do we do it? How do we make the transformation into value chain thinkers? Research conducted by MIT has helped to develop a framework for value chain thinking which sheds light on how to structure and understand the value chain context. We call it competitive value chains. Basically, there are two models of value chains. Model 1 consists of an exclusive supplier network and a more challenging model 2 has overlapping suppliers, frequently key technology suppliers, within a competitor's value chain.

Model 1: Value chain versus value chain model (exclusive supplier network)

Describes completely disconnected supply networks. The whole value chain is highly integrated and connected. Buyer-supplier relationships are exclusive and most supply chain processes such as logistics are specifically designed and proprietary to support the USP.

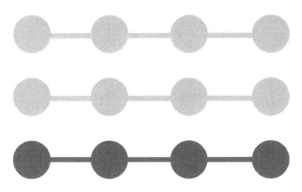

Exclusive supplier network

Example: Zara, 15 days to shop

Differentiation in the fashion industry is difficult to achieve, but Zara is a good example of how to achieve a unique business model. Zara's strongly controlled supply chain is able to respond within 15 days from design to store. How is that possible?

Zara's design teams continuously monitor store sales and keep their eyes open for the latest trends affecting the fashion industry. In this way, about 1,000 new local designs leave Zara's design studios every month. Cuts for manufacturing are then sent around the world and new garments are produced immediately.

The fast reaction time is possible because Zara owns 22 factories in its home country of Spain and about 70 % of its collaborative suppliers for sewing are also located in Europe. This minimizes transport and logistics times and also allows Zara to maintain oversight of the entire garment value chain. In addition, because the collections constantly change, batch sizes are small and overcapacities are limited. Local store managers can then place orders with the Zara headquarters based on their actual needs. In other words, what they order and the quantities are based on local trends and sales potential. On average, each of the over 1,608 stores receives new consignments twice a week and only 15 days after the design and production process has started.

»Digitization comes second – process design comes first«

Interview with Matthias Krause-Uhrmann, Director and Chief Procurement Officer at BP Europe SE

What's your view on Procurement 4.0? Is the digitization of procurement on the agenda of BP?

Everybody talks about the hype of the digitization of procurement with buzzwords like cloud and big data. What I'm missing in that discussion is »process design first«. Procurement needs to design lean processes, drive collaboration internally with business partners and externally with suppliers, align category strategies with business strategies to achieve a stable and performant procurement organization. Digitization comes afterwards. Compared to many other industries, petrochemical is conservative, and most companies do not experience a disruptive change of products as is the case in other industries. Without this kind of external trigger, there seems to be little need to change. However, we urgently need to take great strides to improve our system landscape for a more holistic connected solution – based upon a streamlined set of processes. This will allow us to get more meaningful information out of our data faster. We have dropped our sole focus on »dinosaur« SAP MM and are currently implementing an up-to-date software from the wider SAP product portfolio.

What's your special focus besides digitization?

Most of our business is with non-repetitive projects – so it seems, and in a time of low oil prices. This inevitably shifts our business priority to EBIT-impact measures, meaning cash. We raise questions as to how to improve costs together with our key suppliers. We are quite at the beginning of what others might call innovation sourcing. Simply, some specifications may not perfectly correspond to market standards. We see a huge benefit in working closely together with our suppliers with regard to identifying »creative« cost cutting measures while still enabling the same performance around safe, reliable and compliant operations of parts, systems and processes – sometimes this means just turning specifications into neutral market standards to leverage best-cost-country sourcing opportunities. Suppliers should not be reduced to a cost pool. Our supplier forum is a kind of platform for exchanging good ideas. Internally, we are in the process of establishing procurement engineers to drive continuous improvement. To make all of this happen, organizational effectiveness, process efficiency and data transparency have become key enablers.

What do you see as success factors for the next level of procurement?

Each company is different and needs to sort out 4.0 with regard to their priorities. What's differentiating or particular vs. what is standard and can be leveraged across companies as good practices?
»Safe, reliable and compliant operations« is our top KPI and unfortunately sometimes used as an excuse not to change. The question for us is quite easy: »How do I get all the people successfully involved?« Compared to other risk-adverse industries like aerospace, petrochemical remains behind in terms of efficiency increases next to stable operations. Starting transformation activities to get the commitment of all involved parties is most crucial for a 4.0 discussion in our business. Today, we are still praised for our response time and on-time delivery, while as a leading procurement function we are currently working on »a seat at the leadership table« at all levels and an even earlier involvement in order to ensure a wider set of benefits procurement can bring to the business. Nevertheless, we still

need to change buyer perception from this rather operational role to one which supports business partners in fulfilling their cost and differentiation targets in a more strategic, informed and synchronized fashion.

The aim is to get more out of a pull rather than a push environment with regard to the engagement between procurement and our key internal stakeholders. Key enablers to arrive at a pull situation are the right capability set of our sourcing specialists and an encouraging and backing type of leadership. Next to a state-of-the-art methodology tool kit, capabilities need to include interpersonal and change management skills to engage well, act as a change agent, drive innovation and ultimately manage our cost and risk position.

On top of that, getting in touch with suppliers regarding the development of innovative and creative ideas for improved specifications is a major step forward. In our industry, digitization often follows, but increasingly acts as an initiator and facilitator for excellence in procurement strategy and execution.

Model 2: Value chain companies versus companies model (non-exclusive supplier network)

Describes completely or partially overlapping supply networks. Competitors most probably have some suppliers in common. Suppliers deliver key technologies in more than one value chain.

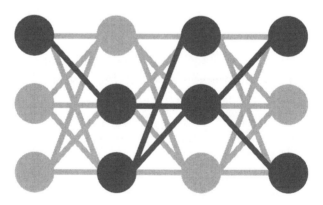

Non-exclusive supplier network

Example: BMW, Audi, OSRAM and the laser light race

BMW and Audi are well known for their premium cars that are equipped with the latest technology and powerful engines, with the BMW i8 and Audi R8 leading the pack. This case study highlights the race that these innovative cars went through to be the first to market. The problem was that both were working together with the same supplier of headlights so there was no possibility of gaining a competitive advantage in the upstream value chain.

It was OSRAM that developed the innovative laser light. Both BMW and Audi wanted to have the first production cars that used these cutting-edge lights.

BMW started talking about laser lights in 2011 but was lagging behind Audi in the field of lighting technology. BMW's chance to become the lighting technology leader was seriously threatened when in January 2014 Audi announced that it would be the first to use these lights in full production models and even presented the technology in a prototype. The battle was on.

Only one month later, BMW declared that the i8 would be the first production car in the world with this innovative lighting technology. In April, BMW said that it would start production of the i8 in November that year. Audi responded by introducing a limited edition of 99 R8 LMX sports cars with laser lights that would be delivered in the summer.

The battle seemed to have a winner until one day in June when BMW installed the new technology in the first eight cars for free but without asking for the customers' permission. BMW made history and finally won the fight with an amazing release event. Furthermore, this venture led to a nomination for the German Future Prize in 2016, reflecting again the innovative power of collaboration within supplier networks.

N-tier visibility – early answers from research

Most companies don't have full supply chain visibility and concentrate on managing their first tiers. But it is becoming increasingly necessary to engage in n-tier visibility.

In the automotive industry all the OEMs are hunting for the best batteries to power their electric cars. Outside the big battery players, there's a small Bavarian start-up called Kreisel with an innovative patented technology that helps get more power from batteries. This is an example of a company that would typically not be listed as 1st tier by the automotive OEMs.

A differentiated view of the supply chain was created by academics almost 20 years ago. Respected academics from a number of universities in the USA (*Supply Chain Management*, Cooper, Lambert & Pagh[1]) developed a well-known value chain model that used differentiated attention for value chain members. A prerequisite of using this model was that it was necessary to know all the members and non-members affecting your value chain. In 1997 this represented a huge amount of manual work, especially when it came to keeping track of non-members.

Managed process links: How analytics helps

Managed process links are those that the OEM finds important enough to integrate and manage.

It is simply not realistic or practical to try and manually map all your value chain companies and process links on a whiteboard in your office. But buyers need to map their value chains and players beyond tier 1. Buyers need to highlight innovation suppliers and further identify make-or-buy necessities to keep the competitive advantages from key technologies. They also need to understand incidents and impacts from changing market parameters and prices in real time. End-to-end applications, e.g. full suites like Ariba and BravoSolution or best-of-breed solutions using an integration layer, combining the value chain network visibility, including the relationships between suppliers, transform a buyer's laptop into a master control station.

Monitored process links: How analytics helps

Monitored process links are not as critical but it is important to the OEM that these process links are integrated and managed appropriately (for example, by 1st tier suppliers that act as module integrators to OEMs).

Monitoring is already a key added value offered by BI applications. First applications are available and all these applications use the same approach. Buyers provide a list of focus suppliers and the BI application regularly sends push information corresponding to the buyer's areas of interest. It is possible to order in-depth reports from some providers if the push information available from unstructured public and commercial data is not sufficient.

Non-managed process links: How analytics helps

Non-managed process links are those that the OEM is not actively involved in managing, nor are they critical enough to allocate resources for monitoring.

A few years ago, in the wake of the Fukushima nuclear power plant disaster, deliveries of electronic parts from Japan stopped for a while. As a result, OEMs recognized that even commodity parts can be crucial. In this case, n-tier visibility is essential. These n-tier suppliers are typically managed by 1st tier module or 2nd tier component suppliers and are therefore usually not on the radar of OEMs. Having responsive tools that give push alerts for all relevant suppliers (according to switching time and cost) allows at least passive monitoring of non-managed process links. Riskmethods and Elementum are examples of providers of such software, which mostly focuses on supply chain processes.

OEMs are aware that their supply chains are influenced by decisions made in other related and competing supply chains. For example, a supplier to the focal company is also a supplier to the chief competitor, which may have implications for the supplier's allocation of manpower to another OEM's product development process, availability of products in times of shortage and/or protection of confidentiality of information.

More and more OEMs have started to screen competitors and their supplier bases.

Value chain designers drive differentiation

The aim of value chain thinking is not to treat all suppliers in the value chain in the same way. Successful companies have a perfectly clear picture of their demand with regard to differentiation-critical demand versus non-differentiating demand. In marketing, conjoint analysis is applied to identify customers' wishes and how people value different attributes (feature, function, benefits) that make up an individual product or service. Other methods like quality function deployment focus on customer oriented design as well. By conducting a similar analysis, procurement can also develop a clear picture of which parts, components and service resources should be allocated in value chain design.

Even procurement functions with a high maturity level lack a structured approach to value chain thinking. Here is a holistic three-step approach to design a best-in-class value chain:

1. *Classify your demand:* The first task helps to separate differentiation-critical demand from non-differentiating demand.
Outcome: Your new focus

2. *Discover your value chain players:* Now outline the value chain step by step – from the final product to its raw material origin. Map your existing players as well as size ratios. If done comprehensively, this analysis supports the decision on where to jump into the value chain.
Outcome: Your upstream supply market analysis, including supplier dependencies and intellectual property

3. *Analyze your value chain players:* Finally, by following a holistic value chain analysis and optimization (VAO) method, a watch list of suppliers that are to be monitored is created and this makes it feasible to scrutinize them more closely.
Outcome: In-depth understanding of your value chain and the opportunities it presents

There are four different analyses that can be performed to give a complete overview of your value chain players.

- *Maximized competition analysis (cost leadership):* For non-differentiating demand, buyers need to know the sweet spot of the competition along the value chain. Global pooling, and in the worst case, forced over-pooling, affected many multinational companies when they built up their global pooling organizations. Nowadays, with a clear picture of cost-sensitive demand, procurement professionals search for the sweet spot of the competition by realizing, for example, that the »sweet spot«, the strongest supply market competition, happens on a regional level and that the strongest competition might also require a shift from module to component sourcing.
- *Cost & risk analysis (cost leadership):* Risk management has come into much greater focus in recent years due to the highly dynamic macroeconomic environment that companies operate in and the fact that the

effects of crises spread more quickly. As well as risks, buyers need to evaluate cost distribution (value add distribution) along the value chain to get an idea of how margins are distributed.

- *Know-how analysis (differentiation):* A deep analysis of where know-how is distributed along the value chain is something that is highly relevant for differentiating demand. Buyers need to know which are the innovative, differentiating suppliers along the value chain. Beyond external innovations, it's not only a question of which companies are the most innovative suppliers in the value chain, it's also a question of make-or-buy. Are key technologies available in-house today or is it necessary to create your own competencies?
- *Product deployment analysis (differentiation):* Changing sourcing strategies can release potentials, e.g. by sourcing whole modules instead of single components. Adjustments of production or assembly processes might need to follow. By conducting an end-product demand analysis, you can find out whether module sourcing is possible at all. Therefore, you need to find out which categories and (sub-) components are affected by the potential module and which business units have demand for it.

»Typical Apple users have to feel comfortable with procurement tools«

Interview with Andreas Abrath, Director and Project Head »Complexity Reduction in Procurement« at BASF

Industry 4.0 is set to change the way we all do business. In terms of Procurement 4.0, is it going to affect what BASF buys?

No, there won't be any significant changes to the purchasing portfolio of BASF. For direct raw materials and indirects we'll continue to focus on high internal value creation. Share of procurement for (IT) services and IP will increase in future.

Will the way you buy be affected?

In short, yes, and in several ways. We've already done a lot in this area to get prepared for the future and how we buy.

There's a clear focus on business partner relationship management (BPRM). The procurement team at BASF recognized that we needed to move away from being a service function and switch towards active demand management. Procurement now has to deal with the drivers and goals of the business and has to turn these into active supplier innovation management.

The process of adaptation in certain parts of the procurement team has already been triggered. For example, the BPRM »roles and jobs« was introduced. This can be seen as »sales in procurement«.

What other areas of your work are under review?

The next areas that have been affected are spend transparency and agility. I'd say that in general the pace at which we do business is accelerating so procurement at BASF needs to be more agile. We need to be able to adapt quickly to changing conditions. This also means there has to be transparency in the processes we use as well as in what's bought. In the context of reducing complexity, this means being able to consolidate faster and to react faster to what is happening in the market.

That is why the key factor is improved spend transparency. There's already a consolidated SAP and ERP landscape, but user-friendliness and data quality still isn't always great. Not all colleagues are SAP experts yet. They need help to properly track suppliers or to analyze order histories and bundling potentials, for example.

What about your IT landscape?

We are establishing a new IT landscape for procurement. This'll be done in cooperation with SAP Ariba to bring about improved SRM, sourcing management and contract management.

We're also looking into heuristic and semantic methods to enhance the material group allocation for purchasing requests and purchasing orders.

Big data and predictive analytics are in the pipeline and will bring about major changes in how we buy. These will be used for more accurate price forecasting and for better evaluation of arbitrage.

We'll be bringing in new colleagues as part of this. They won't just be buyers anymore, but also data scientists.

The overall aim is to gain a better understanding of the internal and external value chain.

Where the internal value chain is concerned, only marginal price changes can have resounding effects, especially on production costs or the shifting of raw materials in the case of shortages. The goal of using big data and predictive analytics is to better identify the reciprocal effects on supply markets and on prices.

With the external value chain we're investing in people and in tools. For example, we'll be relying on the use of business analytics and business intelligence to become more effective at managing our value chains and we're using best-of-breed solutions to automate this.

At the beginning of 2015, the board also launched a group-wide project on Industry 4.0, called BASF 4.0. The goal is to evaluate the opportunities and impacts of increasing digitization and enhanced digital connectivity. The potential ranges from accelerating innovation processes to digital business models for the chemical industry.

For procurement, this means linking BASF's value chain to those of our suppliers. But to be able to create this kind of supplier ecosystem, the willingness to share data will have to increase.

What are some of the main challenges you are facing?

There's plenty going on in terms of Procurement 4.0 and we've come up with some great, innovative ideas, but there is always the risk of failure because of the complexity of BASF. This is why we're now taking small steps and testing new solutions in limited pilots first instead of having big rollouts. This way we can see what works and what doesn't.

When it comes to stronger integration of value chains, the challenge is to find a common technical platform that can serve as a connector or docking station. At the moment, we can only integrate systems in which we have long-term relationships with suppliers. In the future it's going to be important to have a platform that easily facilitates information exchange with all suppliers. Looking at existing safety issues and data security concerns, this'll be quite a challenge.

How is the procurement work environment changing?

Traditional SAP user interfaces are not that user-friendly. In order to give future Generation Y professionals the right tools for the job, we're going to need much more intuitive interfaces. Typical Apple users have to feel comfortable with procurement tools. BASF is working on it with the new SAP/Ariba solution.

There's a certain amount of hype about the use of mobile solutions for procurement. Is this on the agenda at BASF?

We're looking at all relevant trends and technology developments to see what can and can't be used. For BASF, this certainly includes mobile solutions. However, bringing your own device is not on top of the agenda. Concerns on security issues are still high.

Think big: The ultimate scenario for competing value chains

The idea of procurement being a value chain management function with a truly significant impact on the business requires not only a paradigm change with regard to procurement's own perception. It is in fact a huge change management task both within the procurement organization's people and their heads and with regard to the interaction with the business and other functions.

Example: Nutella »strategic insourcing«

In 2014, Ferrero faced serious problems with Nutella, its flagship product. Market conditions for hazelnuts, the main cost driver, deteriorated. It was not only that the price of hazelnuts increased by about 77% from €2,200 per ton in 2013 to €3,900 per ton in 2014, there was also a production volatility of approximately -20% in 2014.

These market conditions forced Ferrero to take action. But just signing framework agreements or similar contracts with suppliers wasn't going to be enough to ensure supply security. Substituting hazelnuts with another type of nut was also not an option because the characteristic taste of the product would change. Instead, Ferrero made a bold move and took over the world's leading producer of hazelnuts, Turkish Oltan Group. By doing so, Ferrero gained full power over the hazelnut market and was suddenly able to control and impact its main competitors, including Mondelez and Nestlé. In addition, Ferrero was able to use its grip on the market to create capacity shortages and influence prices.

Value chain design comes firstly from adopting a value chain perspective, and secondly, from the idea of having a perfect mix of internal and external added value. Therefore, an appropriate organizational structure is the basic prerequisite for procurement as a value chain manager. This means that procurement has to have the mandate for make-or-buy decisions. In this setting, procurement also balances interests of different business functions such as production, which rather likes to keep production in-house and minimize outsourcing.

So in leading organizations, a common organizational responsibility for internal and external value creation – ideally under the responsibility of procurement – is leading to common strategies about in-house core competencies and externalization. Ideally this is linked to the overall corporate business strategy and gives clear implications for resource planning and invest and divest areas in at least a 5-year forecast. A make-or-buy business plan links the overall business plan with the strategy for what to produce in-house and what to purchase in the future. Procurement breaks these aspects down into elaborated category strategies for all major external spend areas.

When it comes to the value chain design itself, active n-tier management is the groundwork. Being first in line or having exclusive access is the name of the game. Especially in non-exclusive supplier networks (think of the example of the laser light race), this can be quite a challenge when it comes to gaining a sustainable competitive advantage. Buyers have to consider not only their module sourcing strategy but also n-tier management. Leading procurement functions contract key technology suppliers on n-tier level that deliver key technologies to a tier 1 supplier. The »all-round carefree« tier 1 package won't do it alone anymore as innovations will come often from tier 2 which are to be integrated on tier

1 level. Such an active n-tier management approach will be supported by automated overviews with real-time information on supply chain data, including, for example, geotagging or news feeds and alerts.

Your survival kit

Before it becomes a »real« business function and a value chain designer, procurement still has some work to do. This is our handy checklist to get your company's procurement function prepared for the transformation.

- Keep the paradigm of cost competitiveness and at the same time develop buyers' mind-set towards differentiation
- Analyze your differentiating and non-differentiating demand
  - Differentiation-critical demand: Parts, components, and services experienced by customers can act as differentiators to a competitor's product. Innovation then becomes the point of emphasis for product management, R&D and procurement
  - Non-differentiating demand: Parts, components, services without any customer experience. Despecification and cost cutting is still a valid objective for procurement
- Extend your view and act as a »business« function: What are your products/services, how can you improve them and support innovation, what is your USP (as a company and as procurement), what is your competition doing?
- Adjust your company's organizational setting with regard to alignment of business and functional strategies, governance structures and cross-functional collaboration to improve the positioning of procurement towards becoming a value chain designer
- Think in value chains: N-tier management is the key to success, therefore develop buyers into value chain designers
- Differentiate managed versus monitored and unmonitored suppliers on tier 1 as well as n-tier level
- Use data analytics tools and services to automatically gather supply chain information of markets, suppliers, technologies, etc.

STOP GROPING IN THE DARK FOR INNOVATION

Supplier management – now and then

Supplier management was in vogue in the early 90s. Automotive OEMs soon followed by the aerospace industry created and implemented concepts to improve interaction with suppliers, but also and most of all to have transparency about the good and not so good players within their portfolio.

Despite the fact that supplier management might be old hat for most of you, there are still procurement organizations just exploring how supplier management could support their supplier relationships.

Before speaking about a possible impact of 4.0 in managing suppliers, we should first take a look at the key elements of supplier management today.

Supplier management today

A classical yet state-of-the-art approach to supplier management is a cyclical process that involves seven different steps: Scouting, selection, qualification, rating, classification, development and phase-out.

Scouting is used to identify potential suppliers for future products if none of those in the current supplier portfolio are suitable. The scouting and innovation team operates in different regions globally to maximize market knowledge and to identify the best suppliers.

Before earning a »ready for business« status, some suppliers have to go through a qualification process. Supplier qualification is awarded to those suppliers that meet all the requirements that show they can fulfill a specific need during a supplier selection.

In order to monitor suppliers' performance and continuing strategic fit, yearly ratings have been introduced which help buyers to make plans for supplier development.

All potential suppliers are classified according to their relevance to strategic aims.

Finally, supplier phase-out describes the process for ending a business relationship.

To allow for more detail, we will focus on the core elements supplier classification, supplier rating and supplier development.

Putting procurement on a solid foundation: The supplier classification pyramid

Many procurement organizations today use a pyramid model to classify their ready-for-business suppliers with active suppliers at the base, recommended or preferred suppliers in the middle and strategic partners on top.

Supplier classification pyramid

Active suppliers that currently lie at the base of the pyramid secure standard business. Some of them might be easily exchangeable. Preferred suppliers have earned extra credit and can therefore be used without further assessment. Typically, these suppliers offer reliable production know-how for products with mature technology. They can also be on the list for future business, for example, if they offer a specific technology, have distinct innovation potential, supply mission-critical materials or because they are the sole source.

Suppliers at the top of the pyramid are usually classified as strategic partners because they add incremental value and offer differentiation opportunities to their client and potentially add substantial growth in business volumes. The relationship with strategic suppliers focuses on future opportunities.

Many companies still rely on distributed responsibilities with a quality management function outside procurement. Disruptive times more often require a fast track qualification to reach time-to-market deadlines. We see an ongoing trend of integrating supplier quality management into procurement.

Supplier rating

In most cases, a preselection of suppliers is evaluated on an annual base. Different criteria are applied. Typically, a performance rating covers four areas: Purchasing, quality, logistics and technology. Assessments are triggered by procurement, but conducted by the relevant functional departments like quality, supply chain and R&D. The outcome is discussed in annual supplier performance meetings with the supplier, but it is also often used as basis for negotiations.

Additionally, some companies conduct strategic ratings for more transparency in business collaboration, integration and operational competence or risk ratings on business continuity and sustainability.

Supplier development

To ensure their supplier base is continuously improving, procurement teams aim to work with their suppliers to upgrade their performance and improve their strategic fit.

A supplier development plan is often mandatory for direct materials and optional for indirect materials, and serves as the foundation for agreeing with suppliers on how and in which areas they can improve.

The way forward in supplier management

Some of you might have the feeling that there hasn't been any significant change in supplier management. The overall process and criteria sets seem to have only slightly changed, e.g. during the economic crisis in 2008/2009 when criteria on »supplier risks« were added to supplier evaluations.

However, when you take a closer look, there are more trends than just that.

From buzzword to common understanding: If done effectively and efficiently, supplier management adds value not only to the success of the procurement function but of the whole company. To make that happen, common understanding and consistent definition of supplier management are necessary to state the importance of supplier management – within procurement as well as company-wide.

Focus on its core: Effectiveness and efficiency imply doing the right things and doing them in the right way. While supplier management approaches have become more and more complex in their initial stages, there is a clear tendency to focus on lean processes. Instead of performing checklist tasks, simplify the process and emphasize the results and how to optimize individual collaboration.

Supplier management should be non-bureaucratic and straightforward – and certainly not an end in itself.

Not one size fits all: Even though some suppliers or responsible buyers are not keen on hearing it: Not all suppliers are of equal importance. Closely linked to the effort related to any supplier management activity, the trend goes towards a more balanced approach that considers the time invested and the potential business impact. Just strategic and innovative partners are treated intensively with tailored measures and activities. All other suppliers are reviewed through a standard process that is reduced to a minimum.

Maximized degree of automation: Times of endless market research activities or collecting and manually entering input in supplier ratings seem to be over – in theory at least. Manual effort can be minimized by using smart applications. Supplier management elements are upgraded with direct data feeds to allow buyers to focus on value-creating activities by interpreting not generating the available data.

»Supplier satisfaction is the key to improved supplier interaction«

Interview with Prof. Holger Schiele, Professor of Technology Management – Innovation of Operations at the University of Twente

»If our suppliers are satisfied, we, as purchasers, did a bad job and paid too much.« This is what we often hear. Now you claim that companies should care about their suppliers' satisfaction with them?

Yes, indeed. I have also heard this comment. However, we can also imagine it being the other way round: Satisfied suppliers run the extra mile in order to stay in business with their preferred customers. Hence, they offer innovations, capacity in bottleneck situations and even better prices. We can find anecdotal evidence for both views. So what is true, or more likely? This is where science comes into play. We have conducted a large-scale survey covering a typical sample of the German high-tech industry – vehicle production, machine building and electronics. We surveyed, among other things, the influence of preferred customer status on a supplier's pricing behavior. The result was clear: On average (with more than 200 firms responding), suppliers would offer better prices if customers were awarded with preferred customer status. The other way round: Standard customers were offered standard prices only. And supplier satisfaction is the first condition for achieving preferred customer status. In conclusion, we argue that buyers have to care about their suppliers' satisfaction.

Do you have an example of this?

An electronics producer decided to implement a preferred customer strategy, selecting one supplier in a particular commodity group for closer collaboration. The supplier ensured its satisfaction with the client; both signed an agreement, with the local newspaper on the supplier's side being present. What happened then? In one product line the supplier immediately offered better prices and got more business. Interestingly, it took two rounds of RFQs till the other suppliers realized that something had changed and one of them decided to react. In the other product line it was even more interesting. The supplier had not been very competitive. So this firm decided to completely redesign its part and in this way, with a cost competitive and technologically superior product, profited from more business there, too. Without – and previous to – awarding preferred customer status to the buyer, this supplier would not have invested in any new development.

You talked a lot about being a »preferred customer«. How are preferred customer status and supplier satisfaction linked to each other?

Supplier satisfaction comes first, preferred customer status second. If a supplier fosters a business relationship, they have some expectations as to the outcome of this interaction. If these expectations are met, the supplier is satisfied. Usually, however, a supplier serves more than one customer. So there is a need for prioritization. Which project do we send our best engineer to? Who gets the testing capacity right now? Whose production do we run in the first batch? Who has to wait? Hence, there is a need to compare which is the best customer, the one the seller is most satisfied with. That would be the preferred customer. From a buyer's perspective, however, one thing is clear: It all starts with having satisfied suppliers. The idea of suppliers lining up outside the door, waiting to undercut each other's prices, so to speak, is no longer the typical experience many purchasers face. Even large firms are small buyers in most commodities.

What would be the role of the buyer in this? How can supplier satisfaction be ensured?

What we ask for is a change in perspective. The buyer has to »sell« his company to the supplier. What does the supplier expect? How can we provide this better than its other customers? This is also the first chance for purchasing to be really strategic in the sense of contributing to the competitive advantage of the firm. For at least 20 years, at each and every presentation it is asserted that purchasing has turned into a »strategic function«. But only because something is important in terms of size – the average industrial firm spends 60 % of its turnover on procured goods and services – this does not mean that it generates competitive advantage. This is only possible if one firm can have better access to suppliers than its competitors. And that is exactly what happens when a key supplier is more satisfied with one customer and serves this customer better than its other, 2nd class customers.

You explained that achieving supplier satisfaction requires a change in attitude by buyers. Changing attitudes, however, is much more complicated than, say, introducing a new tool or filling in another Excel spreadsheet. How do you want to change the attitude of purchasers?

Good question. It starts with small things. Many purchasers we talked to did not even know which other customers their main suppliers were serving. This question had never been at the top of the agenda, and this is not OK. As buying firms, we are competing on the supply market with other buyers. If we do not know all the players and their strengths and weaknesses, it is like a blind flight. Also, when talking to a supplier's personnel or, even better, visiting the firm, »active listening« can be helpful, with the buyer being sensitive to signals indicating what the supplier really thinks about him.

Now, how to convince buyers to change their view? Of course, we can and have to explain the idea, provide examples of the mechanism and on request show tons of research results, all pointing in one direction. However, it has also been shown that presenting and even discussing only reaches a certain percentage of people. Personal experience, doing things in a particular way, however, reaches more people and, then, personal experience is also much more convincing, in particular if we are talking about changing an attitude. So, how do we create a personal experience? One way people recently started to work with is serious gaming. So far, games have been neglected in business training, but also professionals like to »play« and can be reached by this means. For instance, we have developed a serious game in which participants are responsible for purchasing certain materials and are competing against the other players in the game for the attention of a limited set of suppliers. At the end of each round, a supplier satisfaction score is presented so that they can see where their firm ranks – and improve their standing for the next round, then benefiting from satisfied suppliers.

But this implies that you can measure supplier satisfaction. If you directly asked your suppliers if they like you or not, the answer would be quite easy to assume. What do you think?

It is possible to measure supplier satisfaction, though this appears to best be done in an indirect way, indeed. This means that we have to ask for indicators, which typically correlate with satisfaction. If the indicators are positive, we can be confident that the overall picture is too. In order to find out what these indicators could be, we have surveyed a few thousand key account managers. Based on their responses, we could build a model with about 60 indicators to measure supplier satisfaction. We applied these parameters to different firms, and it was interesting to see that there are remarkably stable patterns – regardless of the industry or whether we are talking about direct or indirect materials or services. For example, suppliers tend to prefer customers who grow to those who cannot communicate a vision of increasing turnover. Relational integrity pays off. Tenure with sales personnel tends to be long; hence memories of bad treatment persist. But also operative excellence: Poor processes and weak systems result in a lack of »ease of doing business«, which in turn significantly decreases supplier satisfaction, and so on.

It is nice to know how suppliers regard their customers, but what should firms do in order to benefit from this knowledge?

The ultimate aim is to achieve preferred customer status and benefit from benevolent pricing, privileged treatment in bottleneck situations and access to supplier innovations, in sum: Achieve competitive advantage through purchasing actions. What we have been noticing is that firms, for instance in the automotive industry, start forming »supplier clubs«. A limited number of suppliers are included in such programs to get privileged access to the OEM, for example, getting a contract for the entire series and avoiding annual renegotiations. In return, they have to ensure preferred customer treatment to the OEM and commit, for instance, to presenting innovations first to that particular buyer. Ford is considered to have pioneered such a system, with remarkable success: From very basic scores in the supplier relationship index, they have steadily moved upwards, demonstrating that it is possible for firms to influence supplier satisfaction and benefit from it. So essentially firms have an advantage if they assess their supply base: Which suppliers are really world-class, which suppliers do we need to have better access to than our competitors? And which status do we have with them, standard, preferred or, in the worst case, exit customer? Such an analysis can be the nucleus of a supplier club program. And the basis for all this is to understand whether suppliers are satisfied, because otherwise we do not have a chance to compete for privileged access. Hence, firms would benefit from regularly assessing their suppliers' satisfaction and work hard to increase it. In this way managing supplier satisfaction may well be a game-changing strategy in purchasing.

Components of future supplier management

Looking at how the described elements of supplier management have changed over time, development has been at a very slow pace. Acceleration is definitely necessary to keep on track with ongoing changes in a highly dynamic environment. But how are the elements of supplier management affected?

In a nutshell: The core elements of supplier management will remain the same as a guiding frame. However, the design and implementation of those elements is changing. For example, basic criteria sets for supplier evaluation might remain for a while. Think of an alternative scenario where supplier ratings are simplified following the (already existing) B2C approach. This means a rating based on free text comments and a simple five-star scale. Consolidation of written text ratings to an overall conclusion or even score will be done by text mining applications. Regarding strategic partners, there will be a stronger focus on handling the top of the supplier pyramid with special activities driving innovation-oriented partnering.

Transparency on supplier portfolio and performance: There is a need for a standardized and automated phase-in of new suppliers and regular reviews of the supplier portfolio to ensure work is done with the right supplier base. Transparency on supplier performance can be ensured by an efficient rating system that is built on data analytics and that requires only minimum effort for manual ratings.

Guidelines for buyers: Efficiency in standard processes can be reached by offering buyers a set of standard strategies and supporting instruments, especially for supplier development. Standard procedures apply to the majority of suppliers, hence they are well known by buyers and the degree of implementation is high.

Efficient tools: Standard evaluation activities have to be done or at least supported by big data software that collects and processes the available data. One of the main output requirements for those tools is the readiness of data so that buyers can start strategic work without having to change or process analyses any further.

Additional elements: When standard processes of supplier management are well established, companies can think of additional, rather supportive, tasks which enrich and complete supplier management, for example, market research or risk management as well as financial and sustainability screenings. The use of those elements and the effort involved have to be balanced by the benefits they deliver to the procurement organization.

Strategic partners: The trouble in supplier management is the definition and treatment of strategic suppliers. This means a further segmentation of suppliers that is consistent company-wide according to the logic of the supplier pyramid to identify those suppliers that add value on the top line (e.g. by growth, innovation or integration potential). To maximize benefits from supplier classification, it can be helpful to subdivide strategic partners, e.g. according to their top line potential in innovation and as an integration partner. Other suppliers might cause dependencies and need to be monitored separately. For these different types of strategic partners, detailed collaboration models are established to gain the most from the supplier relationship, which also goes far beyond standard contractual agreements. On the one hand, strategic partners help ensure supply security; on the other hand, sharing know-how becomes more and more important in order to be able to focus on the core business. This is why most of the effort of supplier management has to be put into identifying and managing strategic partners.

Starting with next-level supplier management, you also need to reflect how data can be inserted automatically and used for supplier management purposes. Scouting for new suppliers considers what benefit you can get from advanced analytics, and supplier longlists are generated automatically.

Speaking about automation: suitable interfaces enable cross-linking of your internal systems, external databases and social networks. The overarching idea is to limit operational work while focusing more on the strategic tasks of supplier relationship management. Relationships and especially trust building are supported by system interfaces as well, but it will never make physical meetings, on-site audits or networking redundant. So, despite investments in technical upgrades, also ensure that buyers keep personal contacts and interact closely with the suppliers that were identified as preferred or strategic.

OSRAM – A leading light in supplier management

OSRAM and its new era of supplier management

In recent years, the global lighting market's transition toward semiconductor-based products has been increasingly impacting and disrupting the traditional lighting value chain. As a result, OSRAM made the decision in 2015 to shift its strategic focus and move from being an integrated light manufacturer to a dedicated lighting technology provider with plans to further expand its expertise in chip production and in the area of new applications.

This new strategic focus significantly affects its supplier base, which is why procurement specifically addresses supplier management and also looks at scouting for new (innovative) suppliers as well as end-to-end supply chain optimization.

Illuminating the way to better supplier management

The past supplier management approach provided a strong foundation for the company's global procurement business to be detailed, transparent, holistic and well established within the organization.

The approach to supplier management was already good, not least of all because it was aided by an effective supplier management toolbox. This particular internal tool supports setting up specific strategies for material fields and therefore facilitates finding the best suppliers and better internal alignment between all relevant departments as well as an escalation approach.

However, as is the case with all progressive companies, there is always room for improvement. In particular, supplier classification used a one-size-fits-all approach for all existing suppliers. Clearly, this lacked flexibility as all suppliers had to go through the same process regardless of where they fit into the strategic focus. This increased the administrative burden and took more time than was absolutely necessary, with the inevitable result that the past system was not being fully utilized. In particular, the implementation lagged behind the system's full potential as the rating of suppliers didn't have the necessary prioritization.

OSRAM was keen to get maximum benefits from supplier management as one area of business that is seen as crucial to the company's future success.

Shining a light on the problems

So, what could be done to ensure supplier management played its part? What steps needed to be taken to make a good system better?

Aiming at full system utilization, all potential supplier management tools needed to be pooled and common optimization targets developed.

OSRAM defined the major goals of its supplier management program as follows:

- Gaining business advantages by making its value chains more competitive
- Pooling resources and working with its suppliers on co-creation and innovation projects
- Triggering comprehensive supplier development initiatives so that OSRAM and its suppliers earn greater benefits from the improved working relationships
- Leveraging higher automation of tasks

Supplier management tomorrow: Reloading the original purpose

OSRAM's approach to supplier management worked well — in terms of filling in the required templates and making sure that all mandatory boxes were checked. So a complete overhaul of the system was not necessary — rather a few tweaks combined with improved awareness of why this is all important.

To overcome the problems produced by the one-size-fits-all approach to classification, a modified classification system based on filtered ratings was introduced. The filters in question produce a more flexible approach to rating. This updated method also minimizes the effort needed by the category managers, adding to its usability and appeal. Both the performance and strategic rating remained in the system so that a classification and development matrix can be generated automatically, whereas a new approach was used for the risk rating.

The three layers of filters applied to the performance and strategic rating were instrumental in reducing the number of mandatory ratings and optimizing criteria sets.

A *first filter* selects which categories should be rated. For categories with high competition, simple specifications and low entry barriers, the demand can easily be shifted from one supplier to another. Such categories, e.g. indirect categories, are not shown at this stage. This initial selection is made by business units, not corporate functions.

In a *second step*, suppliers are sorted by their characterization. This filter is used to identify suitable and relevant rating criteria, e.g. depending on supplier life cycle status, shiftability of demand and material type.

A *third filter* is applied to add additional questions within the strategic rating if certain thresholds are reached. The more strategic a supplier is, the more questions have to be answered.

Additionally, two new rating types were introduced, for even more flexibility and independence from yearly rating cycles.

Phase-in rating: To get an indication of the strategic relevance of new suppliers right from the beginning, a short questionnaire is used with strategic- and performance-related questions. Those suppliers matching the defined criteria can be automatically fast-tracked for strategic supplier status.

Project rating: This rating is used to evaluate a supplier's performance in the context of a specific project rather than a long-term agreement. Hence, project-based suppliers can be assessed at any time rather than waiting for the annual performance rating.

Classified and demystified

As a result of the ratings used in the updated supplier management system, changes were also made to the way suppliers are classified. The new supplier pyramid includes detailed definitions to accommodate different types of suppliers, ensuring that they are placed in the right part of the classification matrix. The supplier status is generated automatically in the classification matrix, leading to reduced arbitrariness compared to the previous method.

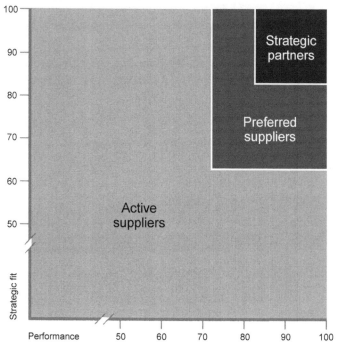

Supplier classification matrix

A clear path to supplier development

Just like the supplier status in the classification matrix, the direction of a supplier's development path is automatically generated in the supplier development matrix, based on the results stemming from the classification matrix. This position is then mirrored in the development matrix to give category managers a general direction for supplier development. The »candy cane« indicates where active development is required and which specific areas category managers need to focus on. With suppliers in the lower right portion of the matrix, category managers only need to keep an eye on particular measures that are usually handled locally.

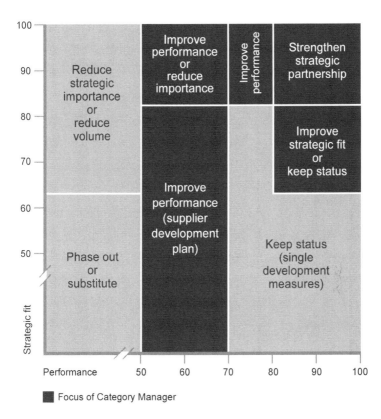

Strategic fit — vertical axis labeled 50, 60, 70, 80, 90, 100

Reduce strategic importance or reduce volume

Improve performance or reduce importance

Improve performance

Strengthen strategic partnership

Improve strategic fit or keep status

Improve performance (supplier development plan)

Phase out or substitute

Keep status (single development measures)

Performance   50   60   70   80   90   100

■ Focus of Category Manager

Supplier development matrix

This added clarity not only aids decision-making about which suppliers are ready for development, it also ensures that the system is more user-friendly and therefore better utilized.

Going one step further, interaction models for those suppliers already on the recommended list were established to give examples of potentially suitable interaction activities, depending on each supplier's status and the specific needs of each business unit. Recommendations are simply and clearly presented as visualizations in the form of interaction heat maps, where activities are highlighted in different colors according to their relevance.

Highlighting the benefits of change

The changes are expected to result in several improvements and associated benefits compared to the previous version of the supplier management process.

Reduced arbitrariness: The supplier status is now automatically generated in the classification matrix, leading to reduced arbitrariness compared to the previous method – by giving the sourcing team the power to change the classification result.

Tailored approach: Bye, bye »one-size-fits-all« approach! Supplier management is now tailored to distinct suppliers and business needs. Classification is more systematic and more flexible. The approach to rating suppliers varies in depth and scope.

Supplier interaction models are differentiated for each type of supplier, but with common core activities.

Focus on implementation: The new approach is to lead to a much clearer understanding of the development needs of suppliers. Today, the focus is on providing the support suppliers need to actually implement the development program.

OSRAM and Procurement 4.0: Some final thoughts

Industry 4.0, the Internet of Things and what is being dubbed Work 4.0 are each individually game-changing trends which cannot be considered in isolation. Each has an influence on the other and it is the cumulative effects that are going to change the way businesses operate and the way individuals work. OSRAM recognized this and saw the parallels across a number of important business functions that are involved in supplier management, such as R&D, quality and sales. Procurement can be the driving force, but cannot handle all changes on its own.

Can we predict the future?

There are intelligent systems to consider. Big data brings with it huge potential for the effective automation of tasks, one of the key goals of OSRAM's supplier management program. But »do we really know what kind of data we need tomorrow to manage procurement even more successfully?« Ulrike Salb, Head of Procurement at OSRAM, asks herself and her team.

Considering the strategic shift from traditional lighting business to »light as a service«, what are, for example, the right KPIs to reflect its future business development, and how can KPIs adequately reflect the phase of its market transition?

In other words, are we in a position to somewhat predict our future requirements?

... and which skills will be required to fulfill this role? Category managers of the future will need the ability to adapt to continuous changes and will face challenges presented by shorter product life cycles as well as the identification of crucial internal and external stakeholders. Furthermore, the decreasing depth of production is likely to mean »less expert knowledge, more network competence« for category managers. Almost inevitably, this will lead the category manager to wonder »where is my place within this network?«

Culture cannot be delegated!

There is a lot to consider on the path to Procurement 4.0. OSRAM is taking a long-term view, not least because, big data and automation aside, the transition brings with it major changes to its organizational culture. Ulrike Salb estimates that these cultural shifts will take between 5-10 years to be achieved as »culture cannot be delegated, it needs to be facilitated«.

»We will raise the relationships with our suppliers to the next level«

Interview with Dr. Thomas Papke, Vice President Corporate Sourcing at Lufthansa

What are your current activities in procurement and how are they related to digitization topics?

Procurement has always been integrated within our IT landscape (EDI, etc.) – digitization in general is nothing new to our industry. We assume that procurement and IT will converge even more, driven by digitization trends in the upcoming years, trends towards more information or real-time data processing.

Procurement has always seen itself as part of the supply chain, but there have never been group-wide standards and tools for purchasers to work with as a basic set. This is now going to change. We want to provide our purchasers with tools so that they can do their job even better. This initiative is about the »purchaser's workplace of the future«, offering a system that provides information about contracts, supplier relationships and status as well as information on market structures and positioning – on your desktop and in real time (or at least in a timely manner).

At the moment, procurement within the Lufthansa Group is developing in two directions. The first one is the introduction of global and company-wide category cluster management. This is done along three dimensions: Market, commercial core processes and local supply management, and requires a strongly standardized and universal process structure. The second one is the development and qualification of employees. Hereby, our focus lies on standardization and internationalization of state-of-the-art job profiles. A transfer of employees can, for example, be implemented by means of job rotation; however, we still see the importance of locality, knowing local market specifics, knowing the culture and, ultimately, speaking the same language.

What are your key challenges with regard to supplier interactions in your industry?

One of our biggest challenges is increasing monopolization or at least »oligopolization« in the aerospace industry along the whole value chain. Hence, a loss of negotiation power is inevitable. Strong global cluster management can provide main levers for negotiations through volume and scale effects.

At the same time, we are trying to get »a bigger piece of the cake« by running activities with our partner companies from Star Alliance and by creating procurement alliances with selected DAX companies.

Nevertheless, negotiation setups are not the same any more. Often suppliers are also cooperation partners or we find ourselves in a kind of »coopetition«, which means that suppliers are clients or joint venture partners at the same time, for example, Airbus as an OEM or Rolls Royce as an engine manufacturer. That's why pure competition is often not given.

In order to raise supplier relationships to the next level, we have to create real win-win situations, and not just »arm wrestle«. We are aiming for holistic optimization of the supply chain, e.g. by means of joint development programs with suppliers regarding the correction of malfunctions (e.g. engine damage). Additionally, we want to increase the innovation potential of suppliers by collaborating with them and ensure their input in new programs; regardless of whether it is for technical segments or for food & beverages.

In ten years, we will have a higher quota of strategic supplier relationships and joint ventures as well as »implants« (on-site services by suppliers or joint ventures). Boundaries between one's own company and external value chains will vanish and actions will increasingly result from procurement networks. As types of purchasing will be diverse, this step towards networking is essential. We will need different approaches and, from time to time, we might even find ourselves being »junior partners«.

Connectivity between suppliers, partners and competitors is becoming crucial. One of the biggest challenges will be to establish an organization which is able to identify, understand and flexibly handle complexity.

Besides a new SRM approach with strategic suppliers – what is your vision concerning business partners?

Internal business partners are often dissatisfied, products change quickly and static catalogs are not suitable. This is also a reason for our procurement alliance mentioned above. Together with Siemens, E.ON and Henkel, we are focusing on tail spend management, i.e. consumables and simple services.

We are working on questions like »How to integrate market prices automatically and in real time« and »How to steer requisitioners and how to offer support for orders via systems«. Another aim is to provide a structured process landscape and tools for ad hoc orders. Under the heading of »Amazon-like interfaces«, users today are asking for appealing and intuitive interfaces as they know them from private life. We are trying to fill the gap between these two worlds, but as we are in a fast changing environment, tools should be kept simple. »Good enough« might be sufficient too.

Engine and aircraft condition monitoring has been state-of-the-art in the aviation industry for 20 years. That's old hat! Regarding big data, we collect a variety of data via our booking and customer data system, which we already use for data processing, e.g. for yield management and price control.

From a procurement point of view, we are closely linked to these business processes, especially to identify demand changes. We see ourselves as part of the company-wide digitization strategy, which is why we are currently not working on the development of »super algorithms« on our own and are not starting a separate digitization initiative. Though, we are keeping an eye on these topics to stay up to date.

Taking all these topics into account, where is digitization at Lufthansa heading in the next couple of years?

Besides this »hype of digitization«, we need to keep in mind that we are situated in a high-security-oriented industry. This means not only being permanently ready for audits, but also includes the topic of cybercrime. Hence, it is hardly possible to transfer applications such as WhatsApp directly to a work environment. Security issues are also taken far more seriously in private life now.

Artificial intelligence has to wait for the moment.

A purpose of supplier management: Finding the right partner for co-creation

> *»In the long history of humankind (...) those who learned to collaborate and improvise most effectively have prevailed.«*[2]
>
> Charles Darwin

Obviously, a close collaboration to the extent of co-creation does not happen with all suppliers. Strategic partners, like integral and highly innovative suppliers, are on the radar of co-creators. Hence, partnership is not an end in itself; it is due to a mutual benefit for both parties. With increasing price pressure, this idea was later displaced by the cost leadership approach.

In a competitive environment, companies need to continuously seek new opportunities to reposition their business, to be more successful and more profitable and – in the end – to survive. Cost leadership is one way of doing this and is an important measure of profit in today's business environment. Innovation and time-to-market are other business objectives in regard to differentiation. Businesses need to reinvent themselves, and find better or new solutions to old or new problems. If you reach a point of diminishing marginal benefits, new opportunities, strategies and concepts should be considered. You might not be able to go all the way on your own. If that is the case, you'd better find partners to join you.

Co-creation is a method that brings different parties together in order to jointly produce a mutually (user-)valued outcome.[3] But be aware that co-creation only generates successful innovations within the right collaborative setting. Let's see what role procurement can play in innovation and in what ways co-creation can boost procurement's impact on the business success.

Procurement is the linking pin for co-creation with suppliers. Procurement must be part of the game whether in finding creative suppliers or co-creating innovations. Sharing sales strategies to create alignment between customers and suppliers creates trust on the one hand and vulnerability on the other. This then leads to a number of questions that have to be considered:

- How do we identify which innovations to go for and which we should drop?
- Can we let our suppliers drive our innovation or how can we guide their innovation and secure intellectual property exclusively?
- Excess innovation leads to waste. How can we reduce risk and waste?

While the idea of innovation sourcing requires a general setup of the procurement organization to be able to identify, contract and implement innovations in one's own company – e.g. the ability to convince or the mandate to decide that engineering and R&D apply suppliers' ideas and innovations – there is also the need to have the right staff with the right mind-set on board. Pure negotiation power plays that focus on savings will not lead to success.

Taking the role of the supplier can be helpful to understand interests and actions. In this context, the preferred customer concept offers you a structured approach of analyzing the relationships with your suppliers.

Example: Trade business

Trading companies sometimes establish creative sourcing teams, perhaps supported by an in-house R&D department, to co-develop products with those OEMs that formerly just served as sources of ready-to-sell products. OEM business buyers are pulled by customers to not only deliver standard products, but also »golden nuggets«, i.e. products that are new and different. Coincidently they have to think about their own brand development.

Pro Idee (proidee.de) is a trading company that uses a business model based on differentiation. Most of the products it sells are not completely new and innovative, but differ in some ways to similar products available from other companies. A great example of this is a canoe made of Plexiglas, allowing the canoeist an excellent view of the fish below the boat – a truly simple but differentiating idea. As Pro Idee is not a producer or product developer itself, this innovation most likely comes from the supply market. Many corporate buying offices of European FMCG companies and retailers are operating in Hong Kong and mainland China with so-called innovation scouts. These are constantly screening local producers for new ideas and solutions, just like a market research function within procurement. Of course, you have to understand your end customers' needs.

Procurement is still afraid of its own innovative power

> »Supplier-enabled innovation is no longer a competitive advantage. It has become a necessity.«

> John Ghaim, Ph. D., Chief Technology Officer at Johnson&Johnson Family of Consumer Companies

Innovation sourcing and supplier-enabled innovation (»SEI«) are current procurement community buzzwords. So why is it that procurement is not driving innovation, or when innovation does happen, it appears to happen by chance? As innovations are often related to technologies or customer-driven wishes, buyers would rather stay passive than risk getting a bloody nose from business partners such as R&D forcing them off their ground.

In some industries at least, progress has been made when it comes to involving buyers at an early stage of the development phase, or using creative formats to challenge existing designs and cost structures. But if we're honest with ourselves, there are very few cases where procurement has played an active role in bringing in innovative suppliers or engaging suppliers to explore new technologies or materials to create innovations.

Some procurement professionals believe that running a supplier workshop on design-to-cost or asking suppliers at industry fairs about their latest trends and features is already supplier-enabled innovation. This does not count as SEI!

A growing number of companies is using scouting software with automated search algorithms to screen the market for new suppliers, patents and trends in other industries which could potentially be transferred to their own. Data crawling across the websites of active suppliers is a method used to identify additional applications to engage suppliers across categories. New suppliers, ideas and technological potential are collected in innovation databases so no ideas get lost and all ideas can be routed internally to the relevant processes.

Another method that is used to support innovation is inboxes. Although this is not completely new, and strictly speaking not SEI either in its original context, it is a way of allowing suppliers as well as start-up businesses to submit their ideas and innovations for consideration. The easier it is for innovations to come through your door, the higher your chances of coming across real groundbreaking ones.

When considering that procurement is *the* function with the most external contact, with eyes and ears on the market, the gatekeeper to existing suppliers and potential new players, should it not also be the role of procurement to take ownership of innovation management or at least to foster SEI? We think it should be.

But how can you make SEI happen? The right way of collaboration cannot be forced but it can be fostered. As of today in many companies, ratings are commonly used by procurement managers to assess the annual performance of suppliers. With this type of hard-factor analysis there are predefined criteria and it is relatively straightforward to see how selected suppliers stack up against these criteria. It's a numbers game. But sometimes numbers are not the best way to help with the selection of a potential partner for business relations, may they be temporary, project-specific or long-term. So-called soft-factor analyses may be more appropriate. Of course, this also applies to hiring new team members.

So let's see what there is to this. Experience tells us that there is no magic formula for judging the success of business collaboration because all partnerships are as unique as the individuals involved. At the same time, experience also tells us that collaboration has a higher chance of success if the people involved share similar values, especially in the integrated and digitized world of Industry 4.0, where human interaction is limited.

How do you choose Mr. or Ms. Right?

How do we identify the right external partner to work with? This is the money question, the one that requires the unfailing attention of the business and specifically the procurement manager. Business partnerships have a higher failure rate than marriages end in divorce. This is a clear warning to procurement managers searching for co-creational partners that they need to be fully aware of why business relationships fall apart and, on the other hand, the ingredients for success. Failing to do this could result in a serious waste of time and money when exploring new business opportunities. The following excursion compares personal with business relationships and gives implications for procurement on how to sustain partnerships.

Businesses don't fail, people do: Excursion into social psychology

It may be stating the obvious, but it's nevertheless worth stating, the most important point to be considered when thinking about collaboration and partnership is to realize that organizations don't collaborate, people do!

According to social psychology research, there are six factors[4] that influence how we go about finding the right partner. These range from looks and appearance, to education, interests, social pedigree, values and finally character. It's an interesting exercise to extrapolate these human relationship traits into the business world, especially procurement, and use them as a guide to finding the right co-creation partner and also be aware that these points matter when looking for new members for your procurement team.

1. Looks and appearance

In real life, beauty is subject to individual perception and tastes and is no guarantee of happiness. Charisma, which entails authority, confidence, and eloquence, generates significantly more attention than beauty.

In the corporate world, an attractive company could be one with a successful track record of development, one that consistently introduces new products or one that is highly recommended by its own employees, e.g. in social media platforms. This could be viewed as something resembling confidence and eloquence. A company such as this may have done well and accrued substantial financial success, which could give it a certain authority.

This can be transferred to the procurement function one to one. If procurement can add real value to the whole business, it will be more accepted by other business functions and will more easily be able to enforce its mandate.

2. Education

Poor communication is one of the main reasons why relationships fail. A similar level of education is advantageous as it makes communication and understanding easier.

In companies, organizational learning can be organically developed from within the organization over time, a common understanding and way of communication being the basis. Additionally, improved education could stem from hiring new talent from outside. Both are of value in terms of providing a solid base from which to start talking and building external partnerships based on understanding.

By enforcing co-creation with suppliers, external communication and understanding will become more and more important for procurement. As its role is generally changing as well, procurement will need people with different skills and other educational backgrounds such as IT knowledge.

3. Interests

A relationship can greatly benefit when both partners share mutual interests. This is sometimes enough on its own to hold a partnership together in hard times. In this way a shared ideology often lies at the foundation of a strong partnership.

In the business world, this mostly means having a common goal or vision. Being in the same industry and knowing the market of the other can help mutual understanding. Having joint interests can be a source of collaborative success.

Within the procurement function, the concept of co-branding can be transferred to co-creation. The development of innovations can get tough if you need several loops until you succeed. Following the same goal and having a common idea of the final outcome can help you through hard times.

4. Values

Values shape how different people see the world. With a common basis, differences can be a fruitful benefit for discussions; however, it is not necessary to share all the same values for an enduring and successful relationship.

In business, not all values are shared. And even if values are shared it is most unlikely that all values are given the same priority. Nevertheless, a similar mind-set on how to deal with one another is necessary in order to foster a fruitful relationship.

For procurement, mutual trust is of particular importance, e.g. when having to deal with non-exclusive value chain networks. It can be the decisive force for securing innovation potential and intellectual property rights and eventually competitive advantages.

5. Social pedigree

Proximity breeds the same values, similar interests and almost certainly dictates that two people speak the same language. In earlier times, couples used to come from the same region. Today, globalization, social networks and supporting technologies have changed this significantly and contributed to intercultural exchange.

In the digitized business world, globalization has caused the same development, but even stronger. How many companies can afford not to act globally or at least internationally? Nevertheless, the proximity of potential partner companies can be enough to help them to relate to each other and build strong ties between teams. A more likely scenario in our modern world is that companies, not being located in the same area, cooperate digitally most of the time and therefore have to take special care when face-to-face cooperation is necessary from time to time.

Especially in procurement, the best-suited supplier is most likely not located next door, which is why best-cost-country sourcing, for example, has gained a lot of attention in the last couple of years. Procurement has to deal with »old wine in new bottles«, meaning known topics like negotiations that now take place virtually instead of at face-to-face meetings.

6. Character

Our perception of the world is created by how we experience it and how we see it through our own eyes, which in turn helps to shape our character. But there are different ways of seeing and experiencing, so as difficult as it may be, we have to accept that another person's perception of the world is likely to differ from our own.

When we scale this up to an organizational level, understanding character becomes even more complex. It is truly the most difficult trait to identify, as every person or organization is uniquely individual. An organization's character is made up of all the individuals involved in it and is by default quite vibrant and prone to change. On a collaborative level, this means that co-creation can only work if there are similar characters in a project setting. However, in the context of innovation, sometimes it might also be fruitful to provoke conflicts in order to get completely new ideas or to find solutions for specific problems.

Trends for co-creation

Industry 4.0 won't turn us into robots

Now, you might ask yourself, what does that mean for business organizations internally in the age of Industry 4.0? Quite simply, the sum of people that work together and hence frame a company over time develop what we know as a corporate culture.

What underlies Industry 4.0 is the trend of automation and data exchange in manufacturing technologies, or machines talking directly to machines via cyber-physical systems. But even though automation and digitization are reshaping how we do business, the essentials of creative thinking and collaboration are still the result of human brainpower. People and their personalities still make a difference so giving the heavyweight topic of corporate culture all the necessary care and attention is critical when you are looking for co-creational partners.

»Culture (...) taken in its wide ethnographic sense, is that complex whole which includes knowledge, belief, art, morals, law, custom, and any other capabilities and habits acquired by man as a member of society.«[5]

Taking a very broad view, corporate culture can be understood by observing and depicting traits and functions that are lived and institutionalized within an organization. This means that selecting the right co-creational organizations in a bid to boost innovation depends on finding the right partners with the right fit. Prudent evaluation will avoid a cultural clash which could inhibit creative and innovative thinking. Just as the expression »beauty is only skin deep« suggests, it's about getting beyond the outer facade of the company and really finding out what goes on inside.

External input for business programs: A strong trend in the corporate environment

If new innovations and fresh ideas are needed, it is very common for a management team to impulsively attempt to develop new ideas within the company to spur business. But what about the less-frequently considered option of looking externally for fresh ideas?

It is fair to say that external drivers can be safely expected to deliver something new and make valuable contributions that nobody had previously thought about. We know that collaborative partners working on co-creation projects help each other to achieve what they could never have done on their own, whether the collaboration takes the shape of a temporary partnership or something that has the potential to develop into a long-term, sustainable relationship.

Of course, there is more to co-creation than just partnership. In essence, it specifically addresses the collaboration between companies and customers to develop new products. Co-creation of this nature can result in a win-win situation because customers get what they want and companies develop tailored products that help to boost business.

This all sounds very good, a simple solution to a persistent business problem. However, for a collaborative cooperation to work, the two companies involved have to develop the business equivalent of an intimate relationship with each other and, as we know, this is considerably easier said than done. It requires a great deal of time to develop the relationship, effort to keep it going, and consistent and thoughtful input from both sides to maintain its value. Just as in life, one-sided business relationships are doomed to failure.

But why make the effort? Good collaboration is as easy to get a grip on as innovation. Some say that in order to be creative and innovative, you need to be free. Others say, innovation is only possible in a structured way. In any case, innovation is what drives our business and remains the key to being successful.

Innovation as a key to success

Innovation refers to the creation of new products, services, technologies, processes and ideas that are better or more effective than those that preceded them. Managing innovation includes tools and methods that allow the parties involved to cooperate with a common understanding of processes and goals. By using creativity to introduce new ideas, innovation management can be seen as a response to stay competitive.

Of course, there are still activities for serial production and ongoing business. However, SEI transforms procurement's role from pure cost reduction to contributing to new products through the active involvement of suppliers. This includes R&D service providers in particular. SEI can be regarded as the ability to co-create with partners to facilitate new product solutions.

Wherever R&D budgets are kept small, it is comparatively easy to explain the need for SEI and why competitiveness and the future of the business also rely on having the right loyal partners working with you. Why innovate yourself if you can also have someone else being innovative for you?

For many companies, SEI is still regarded as only one method of accessing innovation. Incubators or venture capital investments are far more popular. For companies with traditional backgrounds like Siemens or Deutsche Telekom, investments in ideas or start-ups seem to be much more suitable. The risk of confusing the traditional business and process-minded staff with fancy ideas is considered to be too big.

Disregarding the preferences of individual companies, the need to be innovative in order to be competitive is fully understood. There is an increasing tendency to install innovation managers within the organization, and more and more often within the procurement function. »Fast-track« processes are often used to support activities, so they are compliant, but fast is the operative word. »Fail early, fail cheap« is the slogan of some of these functions.

»We're going to the edge – to get our digital strategy ready by the end of the year«

Interview with Jochen Weyandt, Executive Vice President, Head of Group Business Services and Chief Procurement Officer at OC Oerlikon Corporation AG

What comes to mind when you think of Procurement 4.0 and digitization? Accordingly, what hot topics are currently being discussed at Oerlikon?

For us, digitization is not just an IT and Operations topic. It is one that influences the overarching strategy of Oerlikon and the way how we do business. The challenge thereby is that there are so many opinions around. If you asked 10 people, you would probably get more than 10 different opinions on digitization. At Oerlikon, digitization leads to significant changes along the entire value chain.

Regarding our service offerings, we are working on »preventive maintenance« and conducting »early stage« experiments in the field of visualization and augmented reality. Looking at spare parts, our focus is on automation, especially on using new technology to change the way big data is handled. We're challenging our current systems with the aim of generating better data quality. This is supported by artificial intelligence (AI) technology, which we want to expand company wide. For the procurement function, it is our vision to have AI machines classifying spend data and supporting or even creating category strategies with real-time information about market trends, risks, opportunities and supplier information. These machines would be programmed and trained in a way that makes them smart enough to not need any further support by humans.

How are all of these initiatives managed? Is there a digital strategy at Oerlikon?

Of course, all our key stakeholders are involved in digital topics as systemic feasibility and IT security issues are crucial when it comes to the implementation of new tools. But our approach goes even further and we are ready to undertake digital ventures in order to fully use digital opportunities. Beside the fact that we have started to align all key digital initiatives within Oerlikon, it is also our plan to initiate an incubator by giving the dedicated project team maximum freedom to identify promising digital opportunities. Ultimately, all the results of initiatives are to form a digital strategy for the company. Today, we are not there yet, but we are going to our very limits – also from a financial point of view – to have it ready at the end of the year.

Does this new strategy also influence the way suppliers are going to be managed in the future?

The focus was largely on supply markets during the past years. While Amazon-like marketplaces were hyped some time ago, there is now a shift towards value chain management, i.e. enhancing collaboration and communication with suppliers. At Oerlikon, we are deliberately looking little at tier n structures. As we have high production depth and many of our suppliers are big players with their own well-working supplier management, we decided to focus on tier 1 initially. With them, however, communication and collaboration is the key for successful relationships and to ensure access to supplier innovations.

In the context of Procurement 4.0, do you also see changes in collaboration and communication internally at Oerlikon?

Yes, definitely! There is a new generation growing up with totally different habits, perspectives and especially ways of communicating with others. I have a teenage daughter so I see this every day. If I wrote her an e-mail, I know for sure that I would never get an answer. But if I use one of the well-known messaging services, I get a response immediately. Transferred to a business environment, this means a whole new way of communicating.

At Oerlikon, we talk a lot about the digital workplace and how it needs to be designed to suit the requirements of this new generation. We decided on a modular strategy, integrating standard products to increase efficiency and to create an attractive work environment. The idea is to have a kind of »purchasing cockpit« from which you can see all your applications, tools and systems at a glance. Of course, this includes a modern and appealing Internet and intranet presence as well as access to social networks. We've achieved much for the beginning, but there are still challenges we have to face, e.g. legal, IT security and data privacy issues or just an improved user experience like single sign-on.

Taking procurement as a whole one step further, what will it be like in ten years from your point of view?

When I look to the future, I see standardized processes and a maximized degree of automation, which will probably also lead to new ways of working or adapted shared service concepts. Artificial intelligence will be one of the main drivers, nevertheless, any machine will always only be as good as the extent to which we are convinced about using it. All of those changes will be fundamental and significant in terms of changing business models. On top of that, changing collaboration and communication patterns will accelerate our work environment. I'm excited to see where all this will take us.

Building blocks for supplier-enabled innovation

When setting up and introducing SEI, you can easily compare this to baking a cake. It is possible to do this with only three basic ingredients, true to the motto »keep it simple«. You don't think this is feasible? Well, let's find out and try making a »SEI mug cake«.

First ingredient: Supply market intelligence

To get started, you must first identify suppliers with the innovation capabilities to contribute to product development. Such suppliers can be either from an existing supply base or new suppliers, e.g. from other industries. Constant market screenings are necessary to keep eyes and ears open so as not to miss out on any opportunities. A possibility for integrating this task could be establishing the role of a data crawler within the scouting function.

A supplier innovation capability assessment provides valuable support to evaluate the level of innovation within the organization of a selected supplier. Apart from innovativeness and technological strength, open communication and close collaboration are essential to ensure that you're on the same page as the supplier. It's important to align the longer-term business goals and technologies of key suppliers with the need for innovation and the business goals of the buyer at an early stage.

Additionally, supplier innovation performance scorecards can be used to measure a supplier's innovation capability. Suitable KPIs could be, for example, customer satisfaction, brand platform, return on investment, and number of patents or patent applications.

Second ingredient: Traction

The second building block is provided by establishing some rules of the game. Bringing supplier innovations in might require mental flexibility, some money to play the innovation game and speed to make the shift from a new idea to trials and implementation for serial production. In terms of speed, a fast-track and agile process can be the solution.

Governance structures and the responsibilities of both the internal and external parties involved need to be clearly defined. Governance addresses such topics as the setup of processes for external collaboration and the definition of roles and responsibilities in terms of budget and decision-making.

KPIs ensure measurement of progress and success. KPIs on innovation require quantification and tracking of activities related to creativity events and supplier interaction. Examples of such KPIs are number of suppliers with aligned technology roadmap, number of joint innovation projects, implemented design ratio, business volume of exclusive supplier patents and project value by procurement-negotiated supplier-enabled innovation.

But don't overdo it. Creativity and inspiration for innovations need more flexibility and freedom than corporates usually grant business processes.

Third ingredient: Legal

There aren't likely to be any legal issues as long as there is no serious innovation on the table, but once there is, you'd better make sure there is an agreement in place about ownership and compensation, particularly about IP rights, patents and exclusivity. To ensure that both companies create value through successful SEI, new IP sharing models are required.

After mixing the ingredients, putting everything in a mug and some baking time later, you will see that it actually worked out and the result will be your SEI mug cake. The consistency looks fluffy and delicious, but let's take a bite to see if it is also tasty – as, to be honest, the taste is still most important. … Not satisfied and convinced by the cake? Neither are we, so maybe we have to add some more ingredients. The good news is: You can decide on what and how much to add! Just refine the recipe to your taste. All the optional ingredients will only make your cake better.

Further ingredients for an unforgettable taste: Methods

The right methods and tools are needed to support successful SEI. Web crawlers or optimized search engines can be used to support the scouting process. Creative formats for workshops and supplier meetings can unchain the imagination and allow it the freedom to wander beyond normally prescribed boundaries. Lean labs, innovation days, or supplier think tanks, no matter what you call these events, they are most effective when you bring the right people together and ensure an open, inspiring atmosphere. Once your suppliers are bubbling over with ideas, you need to ensure that each idea and innovation is captured. An electronic or even web-based database with advanced functionalities should be looked into.

With this mind-set, SEI is a big chance to bring fruitful ideas into your company – in close collaboration with your own R&D department, of course. Every company can become an innovative company!

 ## »We got the wake-up call some time ago!«

Interview with Martin Austermann, Senior Vice President Group Sourcing at Husqvarna Group

Digitization is said to change businesses and product/service portfolios. What are the implications at Husqvarna in regard to »what you buy« and »how you buy«?

Let me start with a little flashback of the last couple of years. We've put a lot of effort in operational excellence initiatives company-wide. For procurement, this meant typical investments in commodity excellence and programs were mainly KPI driven with a focus on quality, cash flow and cost. We've achieved great results and even won the Procurement Leaders Award for Excellence this year, which we are really proud of. The aim of all these initiatives was to recalibrate our baseline so that we are now able to deliver a significant value add to the company, i.e. a higher EBIT and higher stock price.

In procurement, we have a series of 3-year programs running called Excite. At the moment, Excite 2.0 is running and the last one is planned to start in 2020. With Excite 1.0 we were able to reach a new excellence level by improving our performance. The 2.0 program focuses on innovation, especially on the topic of »supplier-enabled innovation«, where we collaborate with a couple of other renowned corporates. In our industry sales models are going to change from petrol to battery powered engines or towards connected products including new service offerings. This will cause new requirements in the business as a whole but also in procurement and supplier management in particular. Changes to the product and service portfolio will naturally have implications on the value creation of procurement.

Today we still have an old model of involving suppliers, but to meet these new requirements, we need other models of collaboration and partnerships. Therefore, we want to address two key topics. Firstly, we will switch our process to early involvement of suppliers with the aim of identifying tech partners in fields where innovation is necessary and where we need growth partners. Secondly, we will change our idea management internally and externally as the innovation potential of our suppliers is only used to an estimated 20–30%. We have to fill our pipeline, not just with radical innovations but also with smaller, rather incremental ones.

At Husqvarna, we tend to a »not invented here« thinking, which is a problem as we definitely have to open up for innovation. Not only our mind-set has to change but also the skill set of our buyers. They will have to approach markets actively and bring new ideas into the company. Procurement must be able to utilize the full spectrum of its opportunities, otherwise we won't have a say anymore. We have to give structure by guiding what to do and how to do it. This also includes new collaboration models with external value creation, e.g. through partnerships with suppliers, joint ventures or investments in suppliers. Even though our industry is not hit that hard by changes such as shorter life cycles, changes are going to come and we need to be prepared.

Do your Excite programs also handle these aspects from a systems' point of view?

For us, our systems and tools must be able to support substantial category work. Probably the biggest issue is data analysis, but I assume this is still a work in progress everywhere. We will need better forecasts and faster market information in the future. Efficient tools are still missing and people don't have the right skills yet. However, there are first approaches to use predictive analytics, e.g. in travel where the yield management of airlines is analyzed to predict airfares. The findings are then to be transferred or applied to other categories.

What implications do all these changes have on organization at Husqvarna?

Innovation and collaboration are not just topics that affect procurement. It's a rather cross-functional matter where procurement has to make its contribution. We have solid processes, e.g. for make-or-buy decisions, and we are experienced in piloting new projects. But as mentioned, we're struggling when it comes to sharing patents, secrets, etc. with external stakeholders. There are different ways of thinking in the various countries we are located in, so we have to deal with cultural challenges as well. This is also a part of our Excite initiative in the form of leadership development and cross-functional collaboration. Procurement is supported by top management, but we need to improve our standing in other functions. Legal is a good example of where we still have to make a lot of persuasive effort.

In the area of asset management, we're looking at the whole supply chain. Procurement has the knowledge of suppliers regarding testing devices, specifications and so on. The question is on the one side whether processes are properly set up and whether we have second sources where necessary, on the other side whether we are living in a setup of duplications and unnecessarily costly duplications.

Another topic is the division of labor from a cost optimization point of view. Operative procurement might well be replaced by automation in about ten years with fewer resources needed in this area. The remaining ones will have to extend their skills, e.g. in cost analytics, that's why we created a special program for employee development. The »brains in procurement« will be global business managers who have category expertise, know their markets, act quickly and decisively and are able to streamline and manage complex supply chains.

All in all, our well-known KPIs will remain (increasing quality, decreasing costs), but our flexibility in supply chain and logistics will have to grow as we are dependent on seasonal business. This means a need for the connectivity of supply chains and optimization of the combination of online and offline business.

Procurement at Husqvarna has the ambition to position itself as a conductor of existing and potential suppliers in order to secure value creation and differentiation.

The before mentioned examples were more like sprinkles or a creamy topping. If you want to improve the cake batter, you can try out the following methods.

- Procurement key account management (PKAM)
- Supplier reverse rating and preferred customer concept
- Collaboration models, e.g. »Collaboration Bonbon«
- Supplier think tanks and communities
- Innovation days and field trips
- Creativity formats, e.g. design thinking and LEGO® Serious Play®

Key account management in procurement

Not new but rather to be regarded as a classic all-time flavor is key account management. When used smartly, procurement key account management can greatly help the collaborating teams to successfully engage in a joint venture.

Co-creation comes under the umbrella of procurement and by transferring the rationale for co-creation to the value chains there will be a dilution of functions. Cross-functional teams including R&D, procurement, sales, supply chain management, quality, and production work together on modules and will bear significant shared responsibilities. Working within the confines of your own box, within a silo, runs contrary to the aims of co-creation.

Collaboration, by definition, is the key to the success of co-creation as it's people that collaborate and not organizations. It is imperative to enable performance and partnership through proper organization of the teams. Procurement key account management (PKAM) provides the tools and methods to effectively blend and engage people so they can get on with the job of collaborating. Because it has to navigate carefully between overlapping teams and functions, PKAM needs to use a methodical approach to keep everything on the right track:

- Screen and identify all relevant stakeholders
- Draft an interaction model to map out connections, interactions and roles
- Organize workshops with relevant stakeholders to develop ideas and form the right spirit for innovation/co-creation
- Form teams and allow innovation engines to ignite
- Be respectful of all results and allow failure to occur. Fear based on punishment will inhibit innovative thinking and freedom of thought

Understanding the traditional KAM management approach

Traditionally, KAM is based on single interfaces that build up contacts and cooperation between two organizations. Most of the time, sales and procurement people lead their particular teams and exchange information, which is then taken back to their teams for evaluation and elaboration.

Bow tie model

From a perspective looking at the whole system including suppliers and customers, this results in a setup where the two central lead functions of sales and procurement are backed up and supported by their respective teams. Inter-company collaboration therefore happens on a 1:1 basis.

This approach shows that the seller as well as the buyer are separate organizations with their respective functions such as R&D, logistics, quality, etc. Cross-functional collaboration happens within the respective companies. The collaboration with the supplier is channeled through key account management, meaning one person or at most a small team of persons. If there are issues to be resolved, they are escalated from within the respective company to the single point of contact who addresses them with the counterpart from the other company.

On the positive side, this mode produces streamlined communication since information is channeled and filtered by the two lead functions before being distributed to the appropriate parts of each team. It ensures that at one point all information is gathered and distributed; therefore there is transparency on what projects are going on. The streamlined and organized format has a concentration of individual roles within an organizational setup.

However, it's usually not the most effective setup as the flow of information figuratively passes through just one channel and this can become a bottleneck. For the same reason, the 1:1 model produces a potential vulnerability because all the shared knowledge passes through only one interface of each company.

Diamond model

A different format that supports the embedding of mutual competences is collaborative key account management. In this setup there are strong interfaces on an n:n basis, i.e. directly between the teams of both parties, e.g. R&D talks directly to the supplier's R&D if need be. The function of key account management and procurement is building a connection between the teams, »orbiting« between the organizations and catching issues that are not to be solved by the already collaborating parties.

This model inverts the traditional 1:1 KAM structure, which results in stronger bonds between involved stakeholders.

It stands to reason that co-creation teams organized like this have greater potential. For a start, the n:n model brings together and connects all the experts and specialists from both sides so there is a better interface for collaboration. They can communicate directly with their counterparts, rather than working through an intermediary. As we've already discussed, understanding and open communication are both vital elements in all successful relationships.

The challenge for KAM on both sides of sales and procurement is to coordinate the broad contact base and inputs. So this setup is also not a guarantee that all relevant information reaches all people who should be informed. Also, with the strong functional ties between the companies it might happen that inter-company collaboration works better than the internal cross-functional collaboration. And, last but not least, this setup is not suitable for every company and every kind of supplier interaction.

Supplier reverse rating

The supplier reverse rating allows a comparison with competitors of your company. It is recommended that execution is done by a third party to guarantee confidentiality and anonymity. The reverse rating offers a detailed description of results combined with qualitative statements of tier 1 suppliers and it enables the derivation of improvement areas and concrete measures.

External support is usually also necessary to handle administrational tasks (e.g. conclusion of NDAs as a qualification requirement for interview partners) and the mostly large set of interview partners. As one rating cycle spans over about six months and consumes lots of resources, it cannot be done on a yearly basis, rather every two or three years.

In the context of SEI, conducting such a supplier reverse rating shows your suppliers that you are interested in their opinion and that you want to improve your organizational setup and processes, especially with regard to external collaboration. This instrument can foster trust in and the strength of your supplier relationships.

The preferred customer paradigm goes hand in hand with this. It also addresses how the supplier sees the business relationship with you as his customer. Prof. Holger Schiele explained this concept in the context of his interview contribution in the book.

Collaboration models, e.g. »Collaboration Bonbon«

However, neither of the models of KAM is able to map today's complexity of organizations and dynamics of environments. Neither the 1:1 nor n:n mode fits the requirements of collaboration approaches. That's why we developed the models even further, particularly in the context of SEI, and came up with the »h&z Collaboration Bonbon«.

Here, both sides – meaning customer and supplier – form cross-functional teams, ensuring internal collaboration, like the ends of a candy wrapper. These teams come together regularly in the inter-company »collaboration space«, the body or core of the bonbon. It represents any form of meeting or workshop where the relevant people meet to develop a specific topic. That means that each meeting can be staffed differently to suit the target. New combinations of people increase the probability of new ideas and solutions. When not in the collaboration space, each team member is part of his/her organization. This enables a constant transfer of know-how within the company, for best-practice sharing within the function as well as across functions.

All in all, the collaboration space is a nice form to keep the idea of the n:n model, fostering direct collaboration which is not limited to the individual functions but which is the perfect combination of cross-functional AND inter-company collaboration. Ideally, this approach goes far beyond cross-functional collaboration. This result-oriented space team must be staffed with all required competencies and adequate decision-making power to be able to deliver an innovative solution that is ready to be implemented, integrated or rolled out. The space team typically includes people from supplier side, R&D, product management, quality and procurement.

To coordinate the activities in the collaboration space, *collaboration project management (CPM)* is installed. Its task is setting rules for the collaboration space, which should be oriented towards the overall set of rules (see ingredient two of the SEI mug cake), and ensuring that these rules are respected. A key account manager from the supplier side or a lead buyer from the customer side may take over this task (or a combination of both), specific project management is not essential. CPM picks up the advantage of the 1:1 model, which was gaining transparency on what is going on. It can also be the interface to other projects that are running on the customer or supplier side and therefore generates maximum synergies and know-how transfer. Of course, this requires the proper legal arrangements (remember the third ingredient of the SEI mug cake).

As a working mode, we recommend an *agile project approach*. Regular reviews of tasks and progress make this approach flexible and easily adaptable to changes like additional requirements, new input and especially lessons learned. Before each sprint (usually in form of two-week work packages) remaining tasks are re-prioritized and resources assigned. It fits best for projects where intermediate results or deliverables are asked for or if quick wins are to be realized.

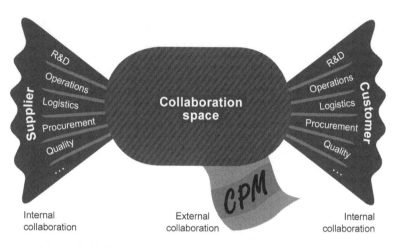

h&z »Collaboration Bonbon« as work mode for co-creation

In this model, the collaboration space is in the center. This is where SEI happens. However, impulses from the companies are necessary and need to be fostered, too. Since this resembles a »bonbon« this concept is named after the sweet. And sweet it is for both sides: One major advantage of this model in connection with innovation is that this supplier-enabled mode gets its own space with one mode of interaction while also ensuring that the know-how of one's own company is integrated. Internal as well as external collaboration get their space.

Comparable models can be already found in practice. The »body« of the bonbon is known as the squad teams, where the teams meet up at a separate place twice a week. »Squad teams« are taken from the armed forces and used as a proven setup to create a solution-minded team. This ensures inter-company collaboration during the present time as well as internal collaboration for the rest of the week. These teams even have responsibility for whole modules and are measured by an EBIT target, following the basic agile idea of creating business impact.

A leading company for machine tools recognized the importance of internal collaboration for innovation. As first mover, the company introduced TPTs, technology and procurement teams, which are responsible for the development of procurement know-how as well as consolidating and aligning technology roadmaps between the company and its suppliers. TPTs can have different scopes of action depending on affected technologies and categories, up to designing technology and procurement strategies that answer the demand of the Technology Council (TC). With this setup, procurement is involved both in TPTs as well as in the TC, i.e. at every level of strategic development. Even though TPTs require rather complex matrix organizations and intensive coaching of TPT members, this collaboration mode is a large driver of innovation if members are sustainably in touch with business needs and supply market opportunities. This internal collaboration model can be extended by adding team members from the supplier side, resulting in extended cross-functional teams (eCFTs) as they can be found, for example, in the automation industry.

Innovation days

When you ask a buyer about sources being used for generating innovations, you most often get the answer that he himself will call the existing supplier base for input and ideas. The concept of supplier innovation days is quite different to this rather trivial approach. In general, supplier innovation days follow the idea of leveraging well-known technical and market know-how from the actual supply base (strategic partners), as well as from other companies with likely relevant expertise.

Concerning innovations, it all starts with the question as to what are the customer needs and expectations. These are not always easy to find out – neither for procurement nor for product development and engineering – though it is absolutely necessary to get focused on the right topics and to avoid a self-centered searching approach. As soon as you have become familiar with the customer expectations, you need to identify the right suppliers, which are often not only the actual ones. Rather, they are coming from other industries where they represent hidden champions or rising stars in regard to your customers' specific needs. Let us provide a concrete example: the customer need might be an improved car sound and entertainment system – user-optimized, with better connectivity, etc.. As procurement of the OEM, in this case, you should not only talk to your classic suppliers of car electronics and entertainment but also to outside players that may come from areas like gaming, game consoles, app programming, industrial design, professional musicians (when it is about sound), or any other start-up with some great product on »entertainment«.

Following that idea, you set the agenda for such an innovation day and invite respective participants to discuss it and workshop with you. It need not be mentioned that your internal R&D, product management, sales and marketing and even production are to be invited as well. And don't forget the aspects of give and take. Those shining stars as well as existing core suppliers will ask what's in it for them! As soon as the innovative ideas and concepts are on the table, you have to be prepared and internally aligned regarding the commitments you want to make or IP issues and follow-up structures.

Field trips

If you have the feeling that your procurement organization is stuck in its notorious environment and that your teams are lacking inspiration, you should think about a trip to Silicon Valley. Many companies have already made field trips there to see how Apple, Facebook, Google and all the start-ups »do their magic«.

Christoph Keese, a German journalist, moved to Silicon Valley for several months to discover the secret of success in this highly innovative and performance-driven environment. He wrote down his impressions in a book called »Silicon Valley« and tried to disclose this secret. Surprisingly, he found out that work and life in Silicon Valley are not as virtual as you might think – it is the opposite! Networks and *personal* relationships count and make the difference.

Such trips can serve as a business driver and new input for differentiation potential. Be open for input from other industries and try to transfer the ideas behind to your respective industry.

Creativity formats, e.g. design thinking

Why is everybody talking about design thinking? And why does Stanford University offer a course called »Project Innovation through Design Thinking«? Should we sign up for it?

Of course, this book was not written to introduce any training programs, but some background information shows the roots of design thinking. It's a method to »better understand problems, generate ideas, and evaluate creative solutions«.[6] Design thinkers do not think problem-minded, rather solution-minded. »Design thinking seeks to build up ideas, unlike critical thinking which breaks them down. Design thinking draws upon logic, imagination, intuition, and systemic reasoning to explore possibilities of what could be, and to create desired outcomes that benefit the end user.«[7]

On the other hand, we talk about co-creation. How do these two approaches build the perfect base for your innovation sourcing or in other words supplier-enabled innovations? Design thinking starts with the end user problems and needs. Combining the idea of co-creation that involves in a narrow definition the user (from firm-centric networks to user-centric networks) in the problem-solving process, with design thinking we would most probably boost the innovation process far beyond today's discussion about material 1 vs. 2, coating 1 vs. 2, rounded vs. rectangular shapes, etc. We would no longer stick to a cost-oriented innovation process within supplier workshops. Ideally buyers start to think like end users and not like »category owners« – just looking at single parts within one's own area of responsibility.

Procurement claims »supplier-enabled innovations« in a world of disruptive technologies. Co-creation is the intended involvement of the end user to give users the experience of being part of the development process – »Creating an experience environment in which consumers can have active dialog and co-construct personalized experiences«.[8] This idea helps! We often experience the »not invented here syndrome« when innovations come from suppliers. R&D needs to be convinced to enter that active dialog and be open to co-construct. Co-creation following that understanding brings internal R&D competences and supplier know-how to the table. Procurement's role needs to change from coming to that table for final commercial negotiations – or in some cases solely being asked to exchange an NDA – to a function that identifies such high potential suppliers and that builds a nucleus for technical collaboration and R&D to »co-construct personalized experiences«. And that brings us back to design thinking. Procurement needs to think in terms of solutions far beyond category demand. The world is changing as a result of disruptive technologies and in many industries internal R&D has huge experience in traditional technologies, but still suffers a lack of competence in a fast-moving new technology. »Software is eating up the world,«[9] Marc Andreessen, cofounder of Netscape, already stated in 2011. This assumption is still relevant according to the statement of Microsoft CEO, Satya Nadella, in 2015: »Every business will be a software business«[10] – a nightmare even for mechanical engineering market leaders. That's a chance for procurement to play a major role in that game to gain or retain competitive advantages and profitability. From an organizational perspective, such co-creation teams are much more than cross-functional teams. These teams need to get a common target and decision power and should operate according to an agile project approach so that they become a multidiscipline ecosystem.

Think differently: Excursion on biomimicry as trigger for innovation

Nature offers a wide fundus of inspiration for innovative ideas. And quite often, good ideas are found by accident or when letting go of trying too hard. Georges de Mestral discovered the principle for Velcro after returning from a hunting trip with his dog. While removing several of the burdock burrs from his clothes and his dog's fur, he wondered what made those seeds so perfectly and annoyingly sticky. While observing the burrs under the microscope, he discovered hundreds of hooks that are able to catch on anything with a loop, such as fur or clothing. The first step for the invention of Velcro was made.

Prof. Jean-Pol Vigneron started working on photonic crystals in insects quite late in his career. In 2007, he was interested in a color-changing Panamanian tortoise beetle. Sample collection was a major part of this research and he made regular trips to the tropics to find samples. One evening, during one of these adventures in the middle of the jungle, he was sitting with a good glass of rum on the porch of a little wooden hut. He was listening to the sounds of the jungle, when something attracted his attention: The light of a firefly! For a while he observed this beautiful spectacle, but then, a scientist at heart, another thought crossed his mind: What if fireflies have found ways to make light travel easily from the inside to the outside of their bodies?

Why would we be interested in how light travels through a firefly? Well, simply because LEDs lose lots of their efficiency due to differences in the optical properties between their emitting material and air. And fireflies have to deal with the same problem. So, let's take advantage of nature's long path of trial and error to see what solutions fireflies have come up with!

These two cases show us how much we can learn from nature, simply by observing it! And, although they are quite similar, there is also a difference: In the first case, there was no specific need for a solution to a known problem. The final product emerged from a close observation, forward-looking thinking, firm determination to reach the goal (it took about 10 years to go to from the initial idea to the mechanized process) and probably a pinch of luck. This approach led to an innovative and successful product that can probably be found in every household around the globe.

In the second case, on the other hand, there was a *known issue* that needed to be addressed, i.e. light being trapped in the emerging material, caused by differences in the optical properties. It is very important to understand that, in addition to the awareness about an existing problem, there was also a *basis of knowledge* on which the idea could be built, i.e. photonic structures in insects having an influence on the light path to create a color phenomenon. The innovation was created here by making the connection between the known issue and the basis of knowledge. The final product of this approach led to an improvement of LEDs through an adaptation of nature's structures.

We can learn from these examples that ideas can be found by observing closely something that seems quite irrelevant – in a first approach – to the final product and introduce innovative points of view into our way of thinking that either lead to a completely new product or to an improvement of existing products.

Creativity formats, e.g. LEGO® SERIOUS PLAY®

The LEGO Group developed LEGO® SERIOUS PLAY® to unlock creativity within the company. Although this product was not designed for co-creation or supplier-enabled innovation, it is a suitable method for building visions for future strategies internally. LEGO® bricks are familiar to many and easy to use. They offer inspiration for metaphors through serendipity and are a tool to express emerging knowledge. »The creative, reflective process of making something prompts the brain to work in a different way, and can unlock new perspectives. In addition, when all participants have a constructed object in front of them, at the start of a discussion [...] this gives all participants the opportunity to set their own issues on the table (literally and metaphorically), and they all have an equal standing.«[11]

The set of bricks can be used within group settings to share ideas, assumptions and understandings or as a check-in method for workshops. This is how the creativity process is structured:

- Connecting participants to what they are going to explore and helping them to understand the context and meaning of the expected learning
- Involving the participants, especially their knowledge and creative skills to create an end product which is connected to the target of exploration
- Reflecting on the end product to reach a deeper understanding of the result and its circumstances and connecting the newly gained knowledge to further explorations

In the context of SEI, this method can support unleashing creative thinking and transforming ideas into concepts, so it is useful for innovation and product development processes. Why not try it in a setting together with your supplier(s)?

KK Wind Solutions A/S: A supplier's perspective on co-creation

There is no magic formula that you can apply to a relationship to make it a lasting and happy one. Different websites, different experts, and different studies will offer different advice and answers. However, when you begin to look through the material it becomes clear that there are common words that are used to describe the characteristics of a good relationship. These include honesty, trust, respect, mutual support, compromise, loyalty, understanding, shared interests and, last but not least, open communication. But what does this have to do with the future of procurement? The answer is, quite a lot.

Look to co-create – it's what all the cool companies are doing

One option that is increasingly important, and something many companies are considering, is co-creation. If you want to follow a co-creation strategy, you need to find the right partner. And not surprisingly, the exact same words that were used earlier to describe lasting personal relationships can also be applied to successful business relationships. To illustrate this, let's look at an example.

A 35-year veteran of electrical systems for wind turbines

KK Wind Solutions (KK) is one of the leading suppliers and innovators of wind turbine controls.

In 1990, KK partnered with Bonus Energy, becoming its sole supplier of control systems. In 2004, Bonus Energy was acquired by Siemens and was renamed Siemens Wind Power. This marked the beginning of a long and fruitful relationship with Siemens.

KK worked hand in hand with Siemens Wind Power as it consolidated its position as one of the leading suppliers of on- and off-shore wind turbines.

Problems are a part of every relationship just as they are part of everyday life. In this case, KK had been focusing primarily on one customer, Siemens Wind Power.

The period from 2006-2010 represented the boom years for both companies during which they doubled their business every other year. This is when Siemens developed a new system, the Siemens Integrated Control System (SICS). This was supposed to be manufactured in the core European market, as well as overseas in the prospering American or Asian wind power markets.

Unleash the power of your people

Innovators operate under a progressive strategy in which they see their organization as a part of a bigger system rather than applying a traditional strategy where a more narrow-minded, individual perspective is adopted. Innovators see themselves as being a part of a portfolio of assets and skills which when combined correctly will drive an organization to be an innovation engine.

KK has nurtured the spirit of innovation within its own business and has also deeply embedded itself and this attitude into its customers' organizations – in this case Siemens Wind Power.

One of the ways it does this is through open communication, a vital element of any successful relationship. KK shares information throughout all disciplines and also integrates the procurement departments to cover the whole value chain. This requires a thorough alignment of the teams on both sides as well as the spirit to cooperate together at all levels.

According to Tommy Jespersen, CEO of KK: »The secret to maintaining a relationship beyond the initial engagement is proper key account management and the merging of cultures.«

From bidder to partner

How to maintain the engagement momentum after the initial euphoria has subsided? The key is to »earning your right to do the job«. KK has pursued a strategy of commitment so that it can rise from being just another bidder in the tendering process to being a proactive proposer of ideas and initiatives. In this way it aims to become a trusted and preferred partner. Such an entrance strategy requires a team with the right skills and capacities that can be matched with the demands and needs of the customer. In other words, KK is not a passive partner. It works hard to introduce something new to its relationships to keep things fresh and interesting and to understand the needs of its customers and the scope of the work

By taking such a holistic view, innovators focus not only on their direct customer's satisfaction and experience, but also on the entire value chain. However, with resources being scarce, especially when it comes to finding and retaining talented employees, supplier relationship management is especially important for OEMs. Necessity means that suppliers will also work with the competitors of their own customers which is why gaining preferred customer status can be crucial as a means of sustainable competitive advantage. In other words, be good to your suppliers and they'll be good to you, or in the context of building a strong, lasting relationship, treat your partner the way you want to be treated.

The next challenge in business

In the wind power industry such as in others, time-to-market is a critical success factor and because of this the market's main participants, including OEMs and well-established suppliers, have been reconsidering their strategies. An example of how KK and Siemens Wind Power have been facing this challenge can be found in a holistic approach to sharing best practice throughout their portfolio. This has led to a dialog between the CTOs of both companies about using systems serving as a standard for the industry. This example shows how a supplier becomes a strategic technology partner and how an OEM is able to delegate product development and the management of an increasingly complex supply chain.

For many years KK worked almost exclusively with Siemens Wind Power in what was a mutually monopolistic relationship for both companies. Nevertheless, they created a relationship where they have grown together and which was done by actively nurturing some fundamental traits.

It is most essential to have the people with the right business mind-set in your organization. When this happens, people talk, relate to one another, and use their networks within the organization to look for value. This also extends towards customers. All the stakeholders have to be able to talk openly.

Think big: The ultimate scenario for co-creation

In case you have not introduced any elements of supplier management yet, you should ask yourself if you really make the most out of your supplier relationships. Try not to invent and implement a supplier management concept with a big bang, rather try to introduce helpful methods and applications to track and monitor your supplier performance. Easy-to-implement cloud solutions are available on the market to quickly ramp-up your supplier management to a scalable base. If you are already fully into supplier management, you should rather ask yourself if you want to manage your full supplier portfolio or build up relationships in the sense of »supplier partnering« and co-creation. Remember co-creation is the method for improving innovation sourcing and supplier-enabled innovation. With co-creation, a picture is drawn of how companies can work together and grow beyond their first venture into a sustainable relationship that affords a continuous innovation pipeline and nourishes all those involved. The aim has to be the development of a setting that allows you to regularly screen your supplier base and the respective markets and to bring SEI onto the agenda of top management on both sides – your company and the supplier's top management.

Innovation can't be forced, and failures sometimes lead you to the final solution for a problem. Not all ideas will lead to real innovation. Not all ideas will make it as far as a product trial. However, there will be a few that will be implemented straightaway and others that will be pulled out at a later time, possibly by other departments or product teams. A first step can be to establish innovation-oriented roles or extend existing roles within the procurement team to identify and manage innovative suppliers (pro-) actively. Remember time-to-market and shorter lifecycle challenges that nearly bring us to the need of »off-the-shelf« supplier pipelines. But also after finding one, continue scouting to know what's going on outside of your company and keep up with new market requirements. A first application to use within your company might be an idea competition or inbox. Think also about introducing an online supplier platform to enhance and simplify communication.

If you want to improve the collaboration within your team or with your supplier, keep in mind that it isn't necessary to change everything. Small adjustments might have a greater impact than you think: Try new workshop formats with your supplier for a start. Or try agile concepts for one dedicated project. Or you might set up regular meetings with strategically important suppliers to find out where there is potential to strengthen the collaboration. Or in an innovation team, try to connect the functions of both sides in order to make communication quicker and easier.

Have a set of traits defined that are of importance to you when searching for a partner, and allow strategic drift to guide you to your target, too. Try to feel the beat of the company you want to engage with. Fortunately, our social, private and corporate networks grant access to so much information that your gathered impressions can easily be proven right or wrong. Key account principles as well as other business relationship models will guide you to the format that suits you best. Invest in your partnership, but don't stop dating. Second source strategies can save your company's life if a partner lets you down.

Finally, you should always remember: organizations don't collaborate, people do. Build up a solid basis for collaboration and strengthen procurement's power by pushing supplier-enabled innovation. Integrate collaboration on the inside as well as on the outside, harvesting a collaboration space approach and innovation-process involvement. Only a balanced mixture of both internal traction and external collaboration will maximize your success in supplier relationships, arising from innovation potential.

Your survival kit

Even as automation arises on the horizon of supplier management, don't be a part of the fully-automated machinery that solely follows and sticks to standard workflows. We see automation as an opportunity to shift resources to added value tasks in supplier management that gives »management« a proper weight, and to harvest the »tsunami« of information – configured as push – into our daily work and workflows. The shift from a narrow cost leadership (savings) value proposition to differentiation in regard to a company's competitiveness extends a 4.0 supplier management approach towards innovation-oriented co-creation. Not merely cost-out innovations are necessary. Rather, true technology breakthroughs, e.g. like new battery technologies aimed at satisfying customers' expectations of the cruising range of cars.

- Inspire your team with a »design thinking« *mind-set* – the users' journey and product touch points are decisive for competitiveness – in addition, successful innovation projects are staffed with team members who are able to think in other roles, in other words buyers need to start thinking like product managers and developers
- Open your organization for a partnership to create value and innovation, define the right selection criteria when pursuing a new partner
- Review effort and value of existing supplier management and focus on value-creating activities, concentrate on »real« strategic suppliers, treat the rest pragmatically
- Have a nose for innovative players, your internal stakeholders and, of course, reward ideas
- Establish key account management structures to support close interaction and mandate cross-functional teams with shared goals
- Establish »collaboration spaces« like »squad teams« for co-creational activities and assign them EBIT responsibility for functionalities, not just for single parts or product components
- Be open for other new collaboration and creativity methods, conduct joint innovation workshops with suppliers and internal or external experts to define new ideas, plan activities and prioritize – this measure will break up silos to form and bond teams and spirit
- Abolish time-consuming, administrative and inefficient process steps and implement flexible tools for automated analytics
- Ensure regular supplier impulses, e.g. by inviting external employees from suppliers to join internal squad team workshops – but don't be dissatisfied with a low »hit rate«.

SOLVING THE 4.0 LEADERSHIP CHALLENGE

It is clear that procurement as we know it is changing in so many ways, driven by the changing business environment and digitization. Procurement is far from immune to these changes. Competing value chains have led to the need for strategic suppliers to be deeply integrated into an OEM's supply chain. Co-creation, with its closer relationships to suppliers and target of joint developments, has thrust procurement into the spotlight when it comes to innovation. These are just two of numerous organizational changes spurred by digitization that procurement professionals will have to deal with.

But who is going to lead procurement into this new era? The answer is that with a new era comes the need for new leadership. Leadership traits that were necessary in the past will be subsumed by qualities that some will find surprising. The CPO of tomorrow will be quite different to the CPO of today.

Are you currently a procurement manager and consider yourself a leader ready to cope with the challenges of Procurement 4.0? This chapter will shed light on what sort of leader you'll need to be. Here's a brief hint – happiness will feature heavily on your agenda.

How it was done in the past

The word procurement originates from the Latin »procurare«, which itself is a conjunction of »pro«, which means *on behalf of*, and »curare«, *to care for.*

Care for what exactly? Naturally, care has to be taken with regard to procurement's fundamental functions of negotiating contracts and prices and then assuring delivery of the right materials in the right quantities and qualities to the right place and at the right time. But surely in the role as procurement professionals there are many more things you have to take care of, and we don't mean the daily chore of deciding which shoes to wear or deciding what to have for lunch!

So what is the contribution of procurement in real terms?

If we review procurement's conventional best practices we can see that essential tasks such as negotiating have been augmented by forecasting, budgeting, planning and controlling. This is a substantial list of important tasks that have to be managed to ensure the procurement department functions as it should. Clearly work has to be assigned to subordinates who are then evaluated based on a job description and specific performance criteria. If you think this is how it will be in the future, you are dead wrong!

High hopes – a derivation of lean-agile leadership

Remember the last innovation competition at your company? Your last team-building event? Last session on error culture? Latest initiative on boosting creativity by setting up a foosball table in the lobby or by placing a gaudy sofa next to a whiteboard? Guest lecture on change management? Latest encouragement by the management board to become a bit more like Google, Apple or any other bright star in the heavens of contemporary business? All that talking about out-of-the-box thinking, about a greenfield approach, about turning customers into fans and employees into entrepreneurs? How about the third major reorganization in the course of just four years? The recent wave of dismissals that has been justified by the need to maintain »competitive cost structures«? The numerous initiatives on kaizen, lean, total quality management, continuous improvement, process management, operational excellence, Six Sigma and, yes, the ongoing hype about Scrum, agile, design thinking that are well on their way to degrading to the same buzzword level as their aforementioned siblings?

Assuming that hardly any of these efforts have ever led and, under today's circumstances, will ever lead to sustainable success, it should be worthwhile getting to the root cause of these desperate activities. It'll probably take no more than the first few minutes of your working day to get you there. If on your way from the company parking lot to your desk you have made one of the following observations, then you're close: 1. Reserved parking areas next to the elevators for management representatives; 2. Business dress codes all around (preferably dark suit plus tie); 3. The guy wearing jeans doesn't take the elevator up to the top floor; 4. Private office with extra amenities for your boss. If no such observations can be made, get a coffee and be confident to see what is needed to trigger your cognitive process during your first meeting: There you will probably find management people coming late, leaving early, taking phone calls, assigning tasks, making political statements.

Is it impossible to create a lean-agile environment under these circumstances? In the short term: Yes. The behaviors described above are means of expression, statements. Statements reflect attitudes that for their part represent values and needs. Here we reach the very baseline of human nature – and the baseline is hard to deal with. Unfortunately, in our case, the baseline conflicts with the lean-agile value system that leaves no room for non-intrinsic motivations which show up in aspirations to status and power. Our personal agendas, our unwritten policies, the constraints of thinking and behaving we set ourselves prevent us from moving the slightest step forward towards agility. Missing the tools? Forget about them: Agile is not about tools – just like lean has never been.

But incompatibility of values is just half of the picture. The other half is enrooted even deeper: in long-term socioeconomic developments. To put it more precisely: In inertia – in our unwillingness to react to change that proceeds gradually. Give a warm welcome to the boiling frog that literally misses its last chance to jump out of water which is brought slowly to a boil! Decoding the picture, the water getting hotter represents the gradual replacement of the industrial society with a knowledge society, while the idle frog stands for our failure to adapt our management style to the new realities.

Scientific management, known as Taylorism, has been the prevalent management approach during the age of industrialization. The concept was built on the premise that management kept ahead of the factory workers in terms of knowledge. This enabled the predefinition of working procedures whose execution was made subject to close supervision. The management style based on this was a system of command and control designed to increase labor productivity. This concept worked more or less fine in the socioeconomic environment of late 19th and early 20th centuries.

However, today the aforementioned premise is no longer valid. The game-changing large-scale emergence of high tech has tilted the balance of power between management and employees on the field of knowledge: Nowadays business opportunities will emerge rather from innovative solutions brought up by experts than from management itself. While this fundamental shift of prerequisites would compel a radically new management approach, we are holding onto Tayloristic logic, running our companies by using levers and showing behaviors that are outdated and have lost their efficiency. To name just a few of them: Target agreements, incentive payments, neglecting outwork, fighting idle time, any form of joviality. Some collateral damage can be found at the beginning of this article.

Does the new balance of power make management redundant? Not at all, but it fundamentally redefines management's role and the requirements for the position. Not by chance the concept of lean-agile leadership, a management style tailored to a knowledge society, is closer to the profile of a humanities scholar than to one of an economist or an engineer; which of course doesn't mean that the latter cannot fill the role just as well.

If you are willing to go for it, here are some principles to lean on: Understand leadership as service to your staff. Remove impediments for your people. Create an environment made for knowledge-based work: Foster transparency, criticism, self-organization, lifelong learning, courage, trust. Human capital is the most valuable asset of your company: Increase it by developing people. Maximize their problem-solving skills. Lead by asking questions instead of giving instructions. Embrace idle time. Allow flow experience by letting people pull demanding tasks and by keeping any pressure away from them. Value individuals and interactions more than processes and tools. Take time for relevant reading – which will be Plato and Seneca rather than your industry journal.*

Still motivated to go agile? As a concept designed for a knowledge society, agile will most probably solve the boomerang topics mentioned above that obviously result from a mismatch of contemporary socioeconomic environment and applied management philosophy. However, this article states that

---

*   For those who are not too much into ancient philosophy, here is some useful contemporary literature that will bring you closer to the concept of lean-agile leadership: S. Denning, *The leader's guide to radical management: Reinventing the workplace for the 21ˢᵗ century;* M. Csikszentmihalyi, *Flow. The psychology of optimal experience;* B. J. Robertson, *Holacracy. The new management system for a rapidly changing world;* D. J. Anderson, *Kanban. Successful evolutionary change for your technology business;* E. M. Goldratt, *The goal. A process of ongoing improvement;* Id., *It's not luck.*

today's agile hype is unfounded and will end up in disillusionment unless we shift paradigms. Applying agile without changing paradigms will cause damage instead of benefit – as was the case before with lean.

What's the essence of it? If you bring a colorful tropical bird to the North Pole it will for sure make a good visual effect. But the bird will still die. So before bringing the bird, you have to make preparations. For these preparations, anticipate decades rather than financial periods.

This excursion was provided by Robert Enz, PhD, who works in the field of lean management for the Lufthansa Group. Being an expert on lean and agile frameworks, he is responsible for the training and coaching of employees as well as for the moderation of lean workshops.

Trends seen in today's procurement environment

The skill set required by the modern procurement professional goes way beyond simply being a good negotiator and the safeguarding of material. Procurement is an art that combines people, resources and responsibilities and that requires passion, dedication, commitment and the willingness and aspiration to make decisions. It is about leading teams (including stakeholders, not only within the own team), both inside and outside the company and about building lasting relationships with suppliers while tending to all other stakeholders' needs and wants.

The procurement professional still has to be a good manager but of more relevance today is being a good leader. There are many references to the transition from management to leadership in modern business literature. For example, *The Type B Manager: Leading Successfully in a Type A World*, by Victor Lipman (2015), strongly suggests that while management has traditionally been considered the domain of hard-driving, competitive, high-achiever Type A individuals, these high intensity traits aren't effective when it comes to motivating employees. In work environments where an increasingly high proportion of employees are disengaged and not working at full productive capacity, Lipman's research suggests new forms of motivation are needed. In fact, it's the Type B individuals, those that are more relaxed, less competitive, more reflective, and slower to anger, who have the »people skills« that better influence motivation and productivity. And successful management, after all, is the practice of accomplishing work through other people.

»Procurement is about to reach new heights as an end-to-end solutions provider«

Interview with Dr. Michael Nießen, Chief Procurement Officer at Deutsche Post DHL Group

How will digitization impact the procurement function at DHL?

Digitalization will have a very strong impact on our procurement function at DPDHL Group. It will change our organization and processes, our technology and systems, our management and our business model. No one can say for sure today exactly what that will look like and how fast it will become our reality, but it is something we will have to prepare for in the coming years.

First and foremost, we need to clarify what exactly »digitalization« means. Right now the buzzwords are »digitalization«, »digitization«, »big data« and »Sourcing 4.0«. Everyone involved in this needs to understand what all these terms mean and what aspects pertain to us so that we not only react appropriately to these developments but also take advantage of the opportunities that come along with them in the best way possible.

In terms of our procurement organization, digitalization primarily means an »end-to-end« approach that is customer-centric. Let's take the straightforward example of booking business travel and its accounting afterwards. If we can offer an independent service to our customers to submit their travel expense reports electronically and independently of the booking – as an automated process – we are actually offering an electronic solution for one small part of the whole process.

Digitalization would go well beyond this because we would be reshaping the entire process – from planning the trip to reporting and accounting the expenses.

This will influence our attitude and approach. In the future, we will define our products and services more from an internal user perspective and therefore need to work more closely with sales, production and all suppliers involved in the value chain in order to respond quickly to changes in the market, create competitive advantage and offer »end-to-end« solutions.

Procurement acts as a hub in this network – as a revenue generator or innovation manager, depending on how you see it. Digitalization can become a major opportunity for procurement in this process.

What about management of innovation?

I truly believe that we can definitely do even more in the future. As I just mentioned, our function as a hub will become greater and we will work closer with all those involved in the process, both internally and externally. If we leverage this role and take advantage of the greater transparency that digitalization delivers, deploy the right tools in order to draw the right conclusions and work together to develop products on electronic platforms, then we will be in a position to identify trends early and drive innovation together with our internal customers.

What will the USP of procurement be in five to ten years? How will its function change within the industry?

Digitalization will deliver a level of transparency that will widen the gap between high and low performers. Suppliers will grow even faster or vanish from the market and we can use data in such a way that allows us to analyze these circumstances differently and understand them better. Our ability to do this will become an even greater USP for procurement in the future.

In this environment of opportunities, procurement will reinvent and position itself by reacting rapidly to changing requirements and jointly managing end-to-end processes as support of the departments. Our procurement is prepared to manage all that.

I truly believe that procurement is about to reach new heights as an end-to-end solutions provider.

Building blocks of contemporary procurement leadership

When we speak of leadership, we naturally tend to think of our bosses. However, what is required to play that role? In a fast-paced continuously changing world, we expect our boss to be as solid as a rock, the go-to person when all hell breaks loose, and the guardian to cover our backs when needed. Aren't these some of the traditional traits of leadership? You bet they are! But with the impacts that digitization is bringing to the way we work, and the changing nature of future employees and their expectations, the modern leader has to have a few more tricks up his sleeve.

An army of asymmetric data artists for the CPO

Information has always been important to the success of any business, but never more so than today. To be more precise, in the world of Industry 4.0, digital technology and the Internet of Things, it's data that is highly prized, or more precisely what's done with it, and that means recruiting data scientists.

Traditionally, CPOs were the masters of information and accumulated vast knowledge of markets, products, their company and the teams operating within it. Experienced managers led negotiations and the teams were there to help with preparations and to provide additional support when needed.

That was in the past. Now, with an increasing amount of data to process, there has been an inversion of this traditional setup. This is referred to as the *new asymmetry of knowledge*, where CPOs and managers rely on their subordinates' expertise and analysis of the market. Superiors still offer guidance and support in critical situations and tough negotiations but it's the new kids on the block who are the new masters of information.

This in itself is a new challenge for the modern leader that will become even more relevant when we consider the demographics of the next generation to enter the business world. The nature of employees is set to change and this will require a change in leadership style.

Personnel fluctuation? Better retain to sustain!

Adam Kingl of the London School of Business published findings in his study called *The Generation Y CEO: The new breed of leader* that some managers may find troublesome. The traditional values and motives that were thought to drive employees are being consigned to history. You'll soon need to dance to a new beat (by the way, dancing involves leading, too) when you hear that 9 out of 10 employees will leave your company within the next five years, while 1 out of 3 will go elsewhere within the next two years. Add into the equation the fact that more than 50% of employees care for the team they belong to rather than the organization itself, that they join companies but leave managers[12], and that employer value factors do *not* include traditional benefits such as bonuses anymore.[13] At this point it should become quite clear that new leadership skills will be needed to persuade employees to stay put. Leadership of Generation Y employees (those born between 1982 and 2004) could be especially tricky.

Armed with the knowledge that tomorrow's leaders have lower hierarchical aspirations, a tailored campaign is needed to avoid the loss of valuable human capital. A key question at this point is what are the consequences of people leaving so early, and how can we secure data and knowledge that is key to our business?

If your folks are happy and satisfied, you must be doing something right, right? Or are they already contemplating jumping ship and you simply don't know it yet? Be aware, think twice and don't fool yourself!

Good employees carry with them value that is hard to quantify and impossible to replace. They work well with their colleagues and develop camaraderie that can positively influence those around them, they have extensive knowledge of the company and its offerings, and have built irreplaceable relationships with clients. If a person like this leaves a company, they take a lot with them.

This is exactly where the modern leader has to step in. Leadership, in its essence, is about motivating, inspiring and taking care of people to preserve and build a competitive and sustainable workforce. In other words, progressive leadership must entail the ability to shape an organizational culture so that it creates a strong feeling of employee job satisfaction. That's it, that's all there is to good leadership! Well, not quite. There is more, but whoever said leadership was easy?

Balance is required to allow for work-life flexibility

The era of the 9am–5pm workday is long gone and it's now accepted by many professionals that they need to adopt a less structured and more agile approach to how their time is used. Thanks to the Internet and smartphones, we are available 24/7, so people can carry their office around with them and work virtually from wherever they are. While there are benefits to this way of working, it also requires careful balance to make sure work doesn't stealthily dominate everything else and the ability to coordinate vast amounts of information quickly. In recent decades, work-life balance has been the major contributor to and driver for high employee motivation. In the 2020 workplace, there will be less emphasis on work-life balance in favor of a shift towards work-life flexibility. This involves multitasking through the allocation of different tasks to be carried out at different time slots so that everything is equally prioritized. There will no longer be defined work time or home time. Instead, there'll be a series of time slots that are attributed either to work or to life.[14]

The work-life flexibility approach will have to be supported by an attitude of freedom and trust on the part of the employer and a strong sense of loyalty from the employee in return. This concept of free rein at work will constitute a new challenge for the leaders of tomorrow, and in particular for procurement leaders when their teams are travelling the world, scouting and tending to strategic suppliers. The boundaries between corporate and private life will be blurred through the fresh input from a new employee blend. Private conversations during working hours will be accepted. Conversely, answering very important business requests during your free time will become the norm. The next generation of professionals will try more and more to make their jobs their hobbies. The »Jobby Generation« will have more agile working styles and will request more freedom in how and where they work.

With all this in mind, we have a key message to all CPOs: Assuring work-life flexibility with all the benefits of individualization and freedom of choice will demand that team leaders give individual attention to each team member, especially when considering potential knowledge asymmetry.

Leadership is the basis of co-creation: The key to unlocking a better workplace

Hopefully by now you're already thinking about ways you can make the workplace of tomorrow the best place to be. Well, as already mentioned above: The future is co-creation.

Sometimes change is for the better, and can set free unexpected potentials. So why not get your team involved in creating job roles for your workforce in exchange for multiple opportunities? We all know well enough that those who do the job are also the ones that know it the best. So why not involve them from the beginning? Following that path, we can ensure that things are getting done the way they should be done. Eventually, it's progress that matters to them and not promotions or titles. A conversation with the focus on responsibility, recognition, learning, and joy might unleash some unexpected energy from your team and help to ensure that they stay where they are rather than looking at their options outside your organization. Co-creation is not only suitable for working with suppliers, but also internally. Such an investment and joint approach can turn into a very valuable asset. Do not turn this into a lost opportunity.

As we already know, retaining personnel is a major part of any leaders' job. But that presents the dilemma of how you're supposed to find fresh brainpower and different skill sets to future-proof your business while retaining existing staff. Don't forget, recruiting is just another form of procurement, so you'd better get on the right track to source your talent before somebody else gets what you want.

The power of your network: Use your social media footprint as the new token of trust

In an interesting twist on the use of social media, some forward-thinking companies are not just using a job candidate's qualifications and experience to make employment decisions, but also the strength of their social networks. What is being termed »reputation capital«, the measure of your standing within your online communities both inside and outside the organization, could be used as a reason to hire a particular person or, for somebody already working there, it could indicate leadership qualities and set that person up for promotion.[15] So social media does not just occupying a large proportion of our private lives, it can also be exploited to serve your visionary organization in the hunt for tomorrow's talent, while beating your global competitors.

Holacracy: A thought experiment for your organizational setup

Before going any further, let's just recap for a minute. We've looked at leadership's role in tending to the talent pool rather than to facts and figures, leaders who allow their people to codesign their own job, arrange work-life flexibility, and who use their vast network and the wisdom of crowds to accelerate business.

If these appear to be strange terms to use to describe leadership, then you are likely to be very surprised by holacracy[16], an approach to self-management which encompasses some ideas that are considerably more esoteric than those we've already talked about. Let's have a closer look and try to understand what organizational evolution holds for us.

Holacracy replaces the traditional management hierarchy with a new peer-to-peer system that is said to increase transparency, accountability, and organizational agility.[17] Authority and decision-making are distributed among fluid »circles« throughout the organization and employees are empowered to take a leadership role and make meaningful decisions.

No hierarchies. Groups that manage themselves and make their own decisions. Sounds like a potential for chaos? Well, maybe not. In 2013 the US-based company Zappos decided to axe all hierarchies, titles and ranks. Tasks and projects were selected directly by the employees themselves. Zappos consigned its former hierarchical power structure to the garbage bin. The impetus behind this disruptive organizational system was the desire to make Zappos more efficient and more able to »deliver happiness«.[18]

The business world is watching this experiment with great interest, especially because agility and happiness are two of the factors that will influence the choice of employer for the Generation Y workforce.

Now let's critically think about the scope and impacts to corporate organizational structure that holacracy presents, just to get a taste of future challenges leaders will be facing.

In holacracy, authority is actually distributed. Tasks are defined and undertaken as employees best see fit. By default, this should lead to fast decision-making as no manager is there to question, validate or overwrite a decision made by the circle of employees. However, the conduct and result has to satisfy the rules and regulations that are instituted by the organization's constitution.

Traits of holacracy should work well in procurement to spur decision-making and spark negotiation power and open the door to new approaches to getting the job done. Creating and maintaining relationships is an important part of the work of procurement professionals. Consistency is one of the essential elements for strong relationships and something that the strategic department of procurement has to honor. On that front it is essential to establish a strong, functional and dependable network with suppliers. Application of holacracy philosophy can already be seen in agile project management or swarm organizations.

»From good to great – we supply for success«

Interview with Dr. Johann Wieland, former Head of Indirect Purchasing at BMW Group, now CEO of BMW Group and Brilliance Automotive (China) Holding

What do you think about Procurement 4.0?

For us at BMW a collaborative network approach together with our suppliers is already a key element of our procurement strategy. Our belief is that we can only be successful if we manage to set up a »professional partnership« with our suppliers.

But what does »professional partnership« mean for you?

It might sound a bit outdated, but professional partnership means first of all to behave and act like an »honorable merchant«. This is one of our most important beliefs and, derived from this, we look for a sustainable win/win relationship with our suppliers. And it is important to us that our relationships are not only a cost game.

Our mandate is: »We Supply 4 Success«. This means that we strive for best-in-class performance in the four disciplines »cost«, »quality«, »flexibility« and »innovation«. All areas are important to us and following this foursome we want to create a difference in collaborating with our suppliers in order to create a competitive advantage for BMW.

What does this mean in terms of working with your suppliers?

With 75 % of added value driven by suppliers, we clearly depend on our supplier network. Nevertheless, we at BMW need to be the driver of our supplier network. We select the partners and drive the collaboration. We reinforce the setup of this network engine and set the pace for success. Therefore, for us in procurement, it is a core competence to select the best partners for BMW.

This sounds like a quite human approach, how do you see »digital« changing the world?

Digitization and big data are important and relevant drivers for improving our performance. They will for sure change the way we work at BMW and they will also have an impact on the way we work together with our suppliers. »Digital« will change the entire business, think of fully automated driving, Industry 4.0, online sales or e-banking. Procurement and the suppliers have to contribute to shaping this future »digital« way of doing business. It's one thing to order what a business department wants. But procurement can also bring in new ideas and better solutions. Keep in mind that most innovations do come from our suppliers.

How does this approach affect your people?

»From good to great« is our approach. On one side, we apply the classical procurement levers such as competition and pooling of demand. On the other side, we've also invested heavily in cost engineering. Today we are in a position that we know the best-in-class cost structures for the majority of products and services we buy. This is a tremendous benefit in working with our suppliers, which is realized by our cost engineers.

The next big thing is to tackle demand shaping. We in procurement want to be able to help shape the best solution. Technical and process know-how is the key in order to be an accepted cross-functional partner. Therefore, we focus our recruiting efforts more and more on people with an excellent technical and process background in their respective procurement area. Commercial procurement know-how is »good«, pairing it with technical and process knowledge makes the »great« procurement performance we look for.

Think big: The ultimate scenario for leadership

Computers revolutionized our world some decades ago, so now daily life is swamped by digitization and artificial intelligence which is no longer the stuff of science fiction. Machines have taken over simple tasks, also in procurement organizations. What happened to the people that previously took care of these tasks? This new era of data and digitization demanded a novel approach to leadership and the development of employees in order to cope with the pace of technological development. Leadership positions in procurement are staffed with people that managed to guide their teams through the emotional challenge of redefining or even reinventing their role within the procurement function.

In this new setting, you can see »data artists« that have the ability to extract strategic implications out of automatically generated data analyses. This type of buyer plays with available data and has by far overcome the point of endless and manual data processing. Therefore procurement employees are trained in data analytics. Leadership is not limited to management functions. Rather, it is embedded in every procurement role that drives and serves as a »catalyst« of collaboration inside and outside the company.

Your survival kit

Being a good leader isn't always easy. Consequently, care for your team. Have a look at what your team needs and what is needed for your business. Is it more responsibility for each person? How about trying a concept like holacracy, not for the whole company or your whole team, but probably for one specific project or within the collaboration bonbon? Other companies also try things like this on a small scale first. Certainly, new ideas like this are not meant for every person and every task, but in some cases it might just be perfect. Start small, with a defined time span and a clear task and see how you and your team get on.

Be honest with yourself: Most of the time employees are expected to be flexible these days. With a mobile and a notebook, many can work at any time. But consider giving some of the flexibility back to your team. What's the personal situation people are in? Find out what kind of flexibility they really need and want. Probably it's not too far away from what is needed for business. Make work-life flexibility not a theoretical concept but something that is present in your team and it will be less complicated and fuzzy as it might seem at first sight. This is for sure: Flexibility will make people more loyal and enthusiastic about your company and most certainly, they will spread the word.

- Understand leadership as service to your staff. Remove impediments for your people. Act as an enabler. Create an environment made for knowledge-based work: foster transparency, criticism, self-organization, lifelong learning, courage, trust
- Balance is good, but being flexible is even better. Find the balance between Type A and Type B management styles
- Be a people person. Engage and empower your people
- Define new roles for future procurement and check required competences with your current workforce
- Derive capability development measures to timely prepare your people for new challenges
- Retain to sustain, e.g. by methods like co-creation. But also be open for new forms of collaboration and project approaches to enable creative thinking and a solution-oriented mind-set
- Data, data, data – data is the new oil. What will change is the processing of data »from data analysts to data artists«
- And, last but not least, don't neglect your network. It might have good advice and support for you in case you need it

»Unleash the power of data«

Interview with Dr. Armin Beckert, Vice President and Head of Supply Chain Strategy & Business Support at Airbus Defence & Space

What's your view on digitization for procurement and supply chain management? Is the digitization on the agenda of Airbus Defence and Space?

Digitalization is a mega trend for society and industry and is already impacting us in all aspects. It is of importance to mention that digital is not fundamentally about tools and technologies. In fact, digital transformation will strengthen our focus on customers and users, driving changes in our operational processes, ways of working, and culture of collaboration.

It is therefore a fundamental theme for Airbus, a question of competitiveness and our way of making the 4th industrial revolution a reality. Triggered by the Airbus Group CEO T. Enders' inspiring visit to Silicon Valley together with the Airbus Group Executive Committee members, the company adjusted its strategy and embarked on a journey which will boost Airbus into a new digital age. Furthermore, the Airbus Defence and Space CEO D. Hoke made it an essential part of the business strategy.

During the past two years, we've learned a lot and the learning continues in an exponential way. Every day, we uncover new potentials for digitally driven businesses and services but also see huge opportunities to disrupt the way we operate and to redefine operational excellence. The key is to »try, fail, learn fast« and to utilize the collective intelligence of our people as well as that of our customers, partners and suppliers. The traditional way of defining and executing »monster projects« with multiyear timelines and millions of euros is being disrupted by speedy proofs of concept and projects driven by design thinking.

Core elements for digitalization within Airbus Defence and Space are connectivity, collaboration, transparency as well as governance and leadership.

Governance

Following the idea of agile networks and collaboration, the initial steps were to give freedom and help people find their place in communities and networks. Given that many initiatives are running in parallel across all businesses, and to avoid having to re-invent the wheel every time, it was important to create an instance which facilitates, creates transparency and »connects the dots«. For this, the role of a Digital Transformation Office was established. Of course, the role has naturally evolved into a governance body which provides guidance and helps develop the capabilities and competences which we are lacking. This organization also drives the digital transformation by providing common solutions to common problems.

As always, it is a question of investing in the right things. Of course, there must be freedom to try new digital solutions and translate them into our business context. On the other hand, the investments need to pay off and before investments are made, the business value needs to be demonstrated. Therefore budgets are made available for allocation to incubator-type of projects and proofs of concept.

Leadership

Our executive management's »walking the talk« is another important factor. Digital requires that we »re-think« the way we operate, »re-think« our products and services, »re-think« the way we are organized and the way we manage and lead. Digital presence of managers and fast communication through blogs and instant messaging have to become normal business life. Leaders and managers should also take sponsorship for proofs of concept and digital innovation projects, strongly promote collaboration, connectivity and transparency and »speak« the language of digital.

I also believe that we have to learn faster than others do. This only works if we allow ourselves and our people to fail. Celebrating failure and sharing lessons learned could become best practice.

Connectivity

We set up internal digital hubs and communities to collaborate company-wide. Networking is key and transparency on ongoing initiatives, new ideas and involved actors is a basic requirement for driving digitalization.

As for people, the connectivity between »things« also needs to be built. We have a huge potential for connecting what we procure, what we build and what we service. By making things digital and connected in an industrial Internet of Things, we can create huge business opportunities which we have to seize.

Looking at your procurement function, how do you approach digitization within this function?

It is obvious that a procurement and supply chain function strategy follows the business strategy and digitalization is a core part of it. As a high proportion of business value is created outside our company by partners and suppliers, we are playing a key role in enabling the business to grow, to remain competitive in the future and to enter into new markets with more digitized products and services. This function also addresses the global supply chain and is tightly connected with programs, sales and all operational and support functions. A digitalization approach can therefore only be done jointly and in close collaboration.

Therefore, it is about applying solutions in the area of the (industrial) Internet of Things, the usage of advanced and smart data analytics of big data in supply chain management, »sensorizing« our products and whatever we procure and sell, maximizing the levels of automation, the creation of networks, new ways of dealing with transactions and workflows – unleashing the huge potentials of data. It is natural that this includes engagement with suppliers and partners.

It is clear that the high volume of data which we have to manage along the global supply chain and the huge volume of external and »dark« data which is still unused today are taking us beyond the limits of what is possible with »traditional« technologies and solutions. And this is not even considering the fact that 80% of all data worldwide was created within the last 2 years and that data generation continues to grow exponentially.

People are simply no longer able to digest the sheer amount of data we have to address today. Even business analysts and data experts require a long time in order to respond to business questions. This has to change.

This is why we are looking into »disruptive« technologies to help us addressing »complexity« and to make the benefits of innovative digital solutions available to all employees. We need new ways of managing data, and the whole company needs to benefit from it, not just a small circle of experts. Of course, new competences and data expertise are required to make all this happen – a reason why the governance of the Digital Transformation Office and the collaboration across functions is so important.

It is worth mentioning that, beyond the »digital hype«, we are continuing to further simplify our »backbone« eProcurement applications and solutions as they are part of the foundations on which the business operates. We will continue on this path, as well as with our intense efforts to improve data quality which, by the way, goes beyond technologies and has to address the human factor.

Talking about humans, it also needs to be understood that concerns and fears of employees and stakeholders regarding a more digital world need to be addressed. Digitalization means change, which has to be properly managed.

What are your main activities in terms of a digital supply chain and procurement?

Automation affects our core transactional supply chain processes which go from our interfaces to sales and programs all the way down the value chain through sourcing, supply chain execution, delivery and services. Special attention is put on source-to-contract and procure-to-pay workflows.

Synchronization of planning processes and information flow across multiple functions is essential to cope with fluctuations along the supply chain. Changes in demand coming from customers or programs or design changes lead to amplified demand along the supply chain which jeopardize the reliability of deliveries. New digital technologies allow real-time information flows, synchronization and constraint-based planning by connecting the planning data models across different functions. Simulation and scenario capabilities enhance the way we plan and change the way we make business decisions in an integrated business environment through digitally-boosted sales & operations planning (S&OP).

We have much more information available than we actively manage and use for decision-making. Digitalization for us is about using all data accessible to us to answer our business questions as well as to get answers to questions we have never asked ourselves. Detecting blind spots, obtaining visibility, ensuring compliance with regulatory requirements along the end-to-end supply chain and anticipating all kinds of risks are key objectives of smart data analytics. This, of course, encompasses all flows of data, parts, products and materials within our four walls and in the supply base, including transportation and logistics.

The question in this context is not »what is the price?« but »what's the price of not knowing«.

Having more people addressing real business questions and providing value to business stakeholders also means reducing the effort required to collect, clean, consolidate and analyze data. We see a significant efficiency potential in this area. Big data, smart data and intelligent analytics like predictive & prescriptive analytics and artificial intelligence are topics which we are addressing these days.

THE TRUTH LIES IN THE CLOUD

Let's be honest, procurement has never been seen as a cutting-edge function. For years procurement professionals have been discussing very conservatively the move from operational materials management applications and have been proud of the simple catalog solutions they created. For a long time they have actively talked about the merits of buy- versus sell-side catalogs and they have been proud of getting awarding solutions for Rfx and e-auction. But can you really look at these achievements as leading-edge science, achievements that fit the 70 % externally added value you are responsible for? We don't think so, and it doesn't have to be that way. Be visionary, and with the digital tools that are available, those of you who want to see procurement move forward can harness the inspiration provided everywhere these days.

A vision of the future: Meet Buyer 4.0

There are few parts of daily life that have not been affected by the digital transformation. You shop, play, and receive your favorite entertainment programs online, you communicate online, find a partner with the help of the Internet, socialize through a variety of networked digital platforms, do your banking online and your children get more and more of their education via digital tools such as tablets and electronic whiteboards. And when you need a break from the stress of modern, digital living, you book a holiday online.

A similar, all-encompassing, process of rapid change is affecting many industries and work functions. People, machines, processes and »things«

are connected and networked and operate in harmony, at least in theory! Data, or specifically being the owner of data, is the centerpiece of this transformation. This is mainly driven by the following IT trends.

- Smart (big) data and cloud computing
- Industry 4.0 and the Internet of Things
- Enterprise 2.0 and social media
- Mobile computing
- Security (interestingly, data manipulation or deletion is the latest form of cybercrime)

The procurement industry has not escaped the change process brought on by these IT trends. In particular, they will strongly influence procurement in two ways: How to buy and what to buy. In this chapter, let's take a look at how to survive in the digital era and how to buy more effectively thanks to the tremendous opportunities offered to us by the digital transformation. It is the »cloud era« that provides the foundation for the new procurement age and creates the blueprint for Buyer 4.0. This will be a fully mobile human-robotics collaboration that uses augmented reality, artificial intelligence and big data analytics. The inspiration for this comes not from the prescient writing of a science fiction visionary such as Isaac Asimov, Arthur C Clarke, or H G Wells, but from American actor David Hasselhoff.

Knight Rider as a role model for today

Some of you will remember »Knight Rider« (1982–1986), the classic 1980s American TV series starring David Hasselhoff as Michael Knight, a high-tech crime fighter. Every crime fighter needs a sidekick and in this case it was the Knight Industries Two Thousand, or KITT, a super intelligent, self-aware car that possessed almost human qualities. Featuring autonomous driving, artificial intelligence and packed full of sensors and a few other crime-busting, high-tech gadgets, KITT was, for that pre-Internet era, the stuff of science fiction.

Today, however, looking back, KITT was truly visionary, a model of disruptive technology and the precursor to the self-driving, autonomous vehicles that are slowly appearing on our roads. Visionary film makers have often shown us the future, just as the creators of KITT did 30 years ago. But in the world of procurement, who can outline the future? Whose visions are going to provide the framework for Procurement 4.0?

The answer is that, beyond the covers of this book, there is no one who is really showing us the way.

Survive in a disruptive world or stay one step ahead

Digitization is not just an enabling phenomenon like the early technology steps in procurement systems that started at the end of the 1990s. It must be recognized as the single most important driver of our future in our private and business lives. It's not just at a corporate level where we need to reflect the disruptive changes to a company's business models. Disruptive technology changes the very nature of all functions that preceded it.

The music industry is a very prominent example of this. The vinyl era lasted almost 100 years before it was superseded by the compact disc. Lasting just 20 years, the CD was gradually replaced by MP3 players (Apple's iPod, 2001) which already started to lose ground to music streaming less than 10 years later (Spotify, 2008).

Think about your own private life. Some years ago, you probably sent postcards to your friends from your holiday destination to tell them how nice it was. Today, real-time connectivity and information make postcards an ancient relict. You collaborate via WhatsApp in real time, while also posting regular updates on Facebook and LinkedIn; your Google app pushes traffic information about your Friday afternoon route while your calendar simultaneously shows the weather forecast; your mobile is a portal that gives guidance into what's going on in your immediate environment, such as places to eat; you also receive push information about breaking news that keeps you in touch with the wider world. Mobile first is no longer a vision, it's a minute-by-minute reality that begins every day with the wake-up call from your smartphone.

Generation X is still calling the shots

But of course not all of us are digital natives. Those among us born before 1980 are digital migrants who have tried to adapt with varying degrees of success to rapid changes in technology and the impact that has had on personal and business life. It won't be too far into the future until Generation Z is playing a major role in business. From day one of their lives, these digital natives have grown up with smartphones and other digital gadgets and experience much of their world through a convenient and ever-present touchscreen. They are less likely to look at paper-based books than they are at e-books and they simply can't comprehend that telephones once had to be attached to a wall via a cable.

An interesting experiment[19] was performed using a group of Generation Z kids. A group of them was put into a room with a Walkman and cassette tape and it took them 30 minutes before they realized that they had to put the tape into Walkman to get music to play. Those of us who are digital migrants may find this funny, but this archaic technology, effectively the precursor of mobile music, was so alien to these kids that they initially failed to recognize what its function could possibly be. Now think of some of the relatively ancient technology in use in procurement today and you begin to see why things have to change to accommodate Generation Z procurement professionals.

Buyer 4.0: Part human, part cyborg?

And this brings us to our digital vision of the future of procurement. In the chapter »Discover your blind spot beyond tier 1«, it was shown that procurement needs lots of information to shape and manage high-performance value chains. An array of digital gadgets, including mobile and wearables, future end-to-end, seamlessly integrated IT workflows, and analytics applications that use artificial intelligence will further facilitate the transformation of procurement. Our version of David Hasselhoff's KITT, Buyer 4.0, will make even standard tasks like negotiations, managing costs, capacities/supply security and quality easier. We're not aiming to create a buying cyborg like the advanced robots we know from science fiction. But human-robotics collaboration utilizing augmented reality already exists – e.g. in production. Our vison is to equip the buyers of the future with wearables and other gadgets designed to help them do their jobs more effectively. Gartner expects an increase in the number of connected devices (Internet of Things) from approx. 6 million devices in 2016 to more than 20 million devices in 2020. Just 4 years later!

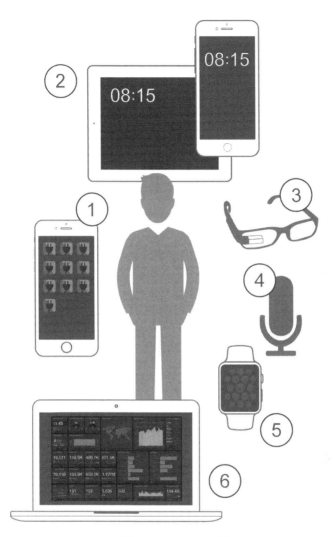

The procurement kit

1. App stores that are offering ready-to-use SaaS solutions
2. Smartphones/Tablets as a standard
3. Headsets and glasses for virtual and augmented reality, like Google Glass™
4. Voice recognition, like Apple SIRI™, Amazon Alexa™ and Google Home™
5. Smart watches, like Apple Watch™ and Samsung Gear™
6. Dashboards/Advanced visualization of analytics use cases

»Speed is the real deal«

Interview with Claus Hahne, Vice President Corporate Procurement at ProSiebenSat.1 Media AG

How do you define digitization at ProSiebenSat.1 and what have you done lately to be prepared for the future?

Generally speaking, we've done much but there is still a lot on our roadmap. For us, digitization is the result of standardization and automation, especially of operative processes, with the aim of increasing efficiency (including effectiveness). We know that speed is one of the key drivers for digitization, however it means a huge challenge for us as our organization is very dynamic and diverse because of the many different legal entities, different business models (media, Internet, production, etc.), resulting in manifold different and fast-changing categories. Procurement will be an impulse generator, i.e. the one to give guidance and to steer the design of tools and intelligent, self-guided workflows.

Our pet passion is the decentralization of operative processes in procurement. We implemented an intelligent system, providing self-guided processes. Strategic and tactical work is done via platforms which offer, for example, tools for tenders or negotiations. Of course, this means that procurement has to define itself not by operative procurement but, amongst others, by the development of category strategies and project management.

What are challenges you're facing right now and have to solve in the near future?

Within procurement, our processes are well established. The next step is to take a look at our internal interfaces, e.g. with accounting and HR. There is significant potential for synergies that we haven't realized yet. For this, we also have to improve our communication and networking, which is not only an internal topic but also affects our relationships with suppliers. One task will be the digitization (as well as automation) of cross-linking and communication with suppliers.

Regarding data management, I don't dare to say we've implemented big data analytics yet, but we have business intelligence that works quite well. In our business surroundings, we see big data as a possibility to create transparency and to provide business units with information. In the first instance, we will focus on content marketing, app programming and creative services. For our catalog systems, we have the vision of a marketplace that is going to be implemented within the next couple of months. Right now, 85 % of purchasing volumes are services which are mainly procured via free-text orders. This is something we want to improve through the marketplace solution.

How does your focus on tools and automation affect the development of employees?

The focus target group of the majority of our internal customers is the so-called »Generation Y«. Of course, we have to offer them an intuitive and appealing work environment, but our requirements for »tomorrow's buyers« have changed as well. We're looking for mutable people, i.e. they have to be specialized in certain areas (e.g. content management or coding), but at the same time have a broad range of knowledge within this area. We need people for classical IT through to cloud, streaming and hosting topics. They must be close to internal business partners and to relevant markets, trends and technologies – in short, they must be on the pulse of the times. There is no need for procurement if we are just an operative processing center. Instead we need team players with strong negotiation competence, people who are able to develop negotiation strategies, to manage projects and to constantly venture something new.

Building blocks for a digitized future in procurement

Procurement cannot ignore a digitized future – answers are needed

Now that we have our vision of the future, the next obvious question is how do we make it happen? What steps do we need to take and what technology can we leverage that will take Buyer 4.0 from the realm of science fiction and into fact. It will require a change of attitude and much more visionary and creative use of technology.

Businesses that hang onto their inflexible IT systems will struggle in the future unless they change and adapt. The same can be said about attitudes to employment. Joy of use, gamification, and user experience are not expressions one would normally associate with work outside the gaming industry. In the procurement business, the most likely attitude is one of »employees are here to work, not to have fun«. This attitude will have to change if we are to attract the best future employees. We are already competing for the rising buyer stars from the current generation, who expect intuitive, lean and simple workflow systems, but soon the next generation will begin entering purchasing organizations.

Think for a moment about how business applications and their use compare to the online shopping experiences we have as consumers. These B2C systems are in fact much more intuitive than B2B applications. Some companies are collaborating with gaming software companies to get insights into user experience design. In other words, they're looking at how to design procurement systems in a way that makes training almost obsolete. Even the approach of using end-to-end connectivity and automation has significant impacts on not only transactional processes, but also on the efficiency of core procurement processes.

A new generation, a new deal

Things will be different again for digital natives. You can't tell a buyer for whom it is second nature to purchase office materials or laptops from B2C online shops to visit a two-day e-catalog training course designed to familiarize them with highly complex and non-intuitive B2B sourcing platforms and systems. And what about getting product evaluations within the purchasing workflow and having full price transparency by showing alternative sources? Shouldn't that be a benchmark for B2B?

On the other hand, there are traditional and highly knowledgeable buyers who know all the tricks in materials management systems. It's going to be a huge leadership and transformation challenge to bring both parties together in a new procurement system. To help address these challenges, it's worth looking at some of the trends affecting the categorization of procurement leaders and those influencing core and supporting procurement systems. In other words, let's take a look at some of the amazing gadgets and tools that Buyer 4.0 will need. The apps linked to the trends in procurement give us a window on the future.

Get your applications in a buyer app store

We do not see a future dominated by robots or even cyborgs, but a future where it's still all about people. People will remain in the foreground but they will be backed by an array of user-centric apps that will provide a level of support and mobility unprecedented in the procurement business. The newly gained freedom inherent in the use of these apps will be used to create added value as they help to enable an increase of creativity in thought and action. The digital native generation is used to customizing their mobiles phones to suit their own needs and even the digital migrants among us more or less do the same thing. However, business applications are still far away from offering the same level of customization. While some providers offer SaaS apps available on Android or iOS platforms, or in the Amazon Web Services marketplace, in reality, many companies still suffer from the legacy of huge, complex, monolithic software structures grown over decades, similar to a plate of spaghetti with regard to the IT architecture and interfaces.

Think about it for a moment. What's the first thing you do with a new smartphone? You customize it by downloading your preferred apps and then rearrange the interface so that it reflects your interests. Why can't we use this user-oriented philosophy for procurement applications?

Procurement needs to move away from the unwieldy IT, the application architecture and software that currently dominates the business and move towards more flexible small business applications (that are connected end to end via an integration platform/layer along with other back-end (ERP) systems, business warehouse, cloud, Hadoop etc.). A look at the different needs of buyers highlights the need for flexibility. For example, operational buyers, who require cloud-based purchase-to-pay solutions, have different demands to buyers, whose focus is on analytics, Rfx, negotiations and contracting. At the same time, project buyers ideally want collaboration tools while for some procurement managers an approval app is enough. Looking into the future, the vision for procurement is task related, where different apps are easily integrated and cater to the various role profiles intuitively and offer buyers what they need for their specific jobs.

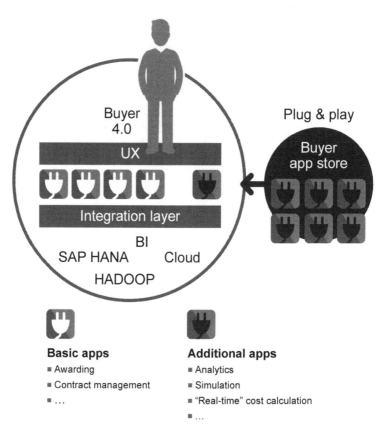

Basic and additional apps

The goal is to provide each buyer a basic set of apps and additional role-specific apps to be added. In the same way as you get e-mail, a calendar and a web browser as standard apps on a smartphone, additional apps can be added that are relevant to a user's profile or, in business, to his role in the company. There are apps available for almost every specific category imaginable, such as awarding and management of construction work projects, simulation of freight awarding, calculation of performance contracting figures, simulation of cost impact in real time based on supplier information and/or market data and so on. There is even a lever analysis app for buyers, like the Bull's Eye app (see figure »Chart list:

Your top 10 apps today« later in the book). There are initial procurement organizations that have their own app developer.

Trends for »core« and »support« systems

Enjoy procurement systems with user experience

Coming from real expert systems in the past we called front end, today we have a completely new understanding of the usability and simplicity of (procurement) systems (see Trends for »core« and »support« systems). We are all used to self-explanatory workflows and interfaces for which we don't need any training or even lengthy on-boarding. Today we talk about user experience, user-centricity and even business applications are oriented towards the intuitive logic of computer games. Gamification and joy of use are buzzwords that not all digital migrants are familiar with. Visualization tools have been significantly improved and allow drilling down, analyzing and discussing combined data from internal and external sources better than ever before.

Focus on value-added tasks by means of end-to-end application landscape

A survey of procurement leaders in 2014[20] revealed that purchase to pay, spend analytics and e-sourcing (source to contracts) are the most digitized processes currently used in procurement. Support systems offering end-to-end connectivity to the core system are a huge step forward compared to what preceded them. They aren't just useful for transferring prices from contracts to ERP systems, but also provide a life cycle perspective on parts and suppliers. Contracts previously stored on paper and primarily generated before the start of production, which changed over the product life cycle, will be stored in a central database in the future including a Google-like search functionality. Many struggle with paper-based storage or even with simply scanned documents in a database that covers a 20- to 30-year time frame (including spare parts after end of life) due to the fact that many different buyers have been responsible for different things during that time frame. End-to-end connected Rfx and contract management systems will prevent information gaps that might happen in cases of claims from suppliers or customers. Each contract awarded can be automatically checked for its impact on existing contracts.

Besides contract management, Buyer 4.0 will need to have access to real-time supplier performance ratings during the awarding process. For example, alternative suppliers, including their rating, can be proposed by the system during the awarding process and can be allocated to the awarding supplier by means of drag and drop. Text search apps look for issue patterns in unstructured audit data as well as internal and external big data in the web and other databases. Supply risk impact, including single country risks, are checked in real time by the system. Such close integration is technologically old-fashioned, but not yet standard in procurement circles. The reasons for this can be found in the complex legacy systems and interfaces which still use a manual Rfx process and standalone, completely disconnected e-sourcing events supported by e-auctioning and simulation systems.

There are several sides to automation. Consider purchase orders that use text-based automated allocation of spend categories instead of having to manually choose the categories, which brings with it the real danger of incorrect allocations. Consider automated reports for sourcing boards and sourcing decisions. Consider automated offer comparisons, including simulations based on designed and defined frame conditions. Consider automated, artificial intelligence-based negotiation (robotics).

Example: Automated demand mapping

Will artificial intelligence replace bundling in global category management organizations?

A state-of-the-art procurement function that operates worldwide is based on global, regional and local category management organization with category-specific collaboration models. IT support is given via retrospective spend management tools, which get the previous period's spend figures about who bought what from whom, in which quantity, and at what price. Buyers rarely have the luxury of complete transparency about upcoming demand worldwide. In the future, IT systems will support the mapping of global, regional and local demand, or the entire mapping process will be done using artificial intelligence. This will change the role of today's buyer in the future.

Be a buyer everywhere: Mobile first

Mobile technology will have a major impact on procurement. Buyer 4.0 will be able to sit in on negotiations where wearables offer simulations and counter arguments, automatically reacting to what the salesperson on the other side of the table is saying. We're not yet at that stage but mobile devices such as tablets are already in place in many companies and, for example, managers really like being able to approve purchase orders on their smartphones while waiting at the airport to board their plane.

From a world where information was scarce and hard to gather, we now live in a world in which information is so abundant that it has become a real challenge to use correctly and avoiding spam-like push alerts. Search engines have brought their inventors fame and fortune because they provide the means to delve into this mass of information and channel the most relevant items. Procurement also collects quantities of data through the increasing digitization of its activities that were unheard of even 10 years ago. Opportunities for using that data are huge: Hidden among this vast amount of data are market trends and early warnings just waiting to be spotted. Good management of this data can generate value. Social media is, in this case, another source of information containing a mixture of opinions and facts.

Analytics goes beyond spend figure dashboards. It's about being best prepared for Rfx and negotiations and getting all the necessary information for designing performant category strategies. There are analytics apps offering promising support that work even as a stand-alone solution. But others are most powerful when they have full connectivity and integration into workflows like Rfx – just consider seamless simulation functionalities within the offer comparison process.

Analytics & collaboration: Effectiveness boost

The ever-growing flow of data hides important information behind a veil. The need to understand the underlying evolutions and differentiate between real trends and ambient noise will be of paramount importance to strategic buyers. They have the challenge of making capital decisions in their category strategy development based on the clarity of the facts and figures they have in front of them. A 2012 article in the Harvard Business Review stated that »Every 14 minutes, somewhere in the world an advertising executive strides on stage with the same breathless declaration: Data is the new oil!«[21] Some do not accept that message but on the other hand, there are some forward-thinking business people who are already of that mind-set and prepared to make the changes necessary to harvest data. However, before this happens, there are several questions that have to be answered. What data do we need and want to share? Who is the owner? What are the ethical issues surrounding increased personal transparency? The answers to these questions can be complex, but overall there are many examples of companies gaining added value from actively managing and leveraging »data lakes«.

In the past we as procurement did KPI reporting and now move to advanced analytics. Historically, business intelligence providers focused on data discovery, data mining and demand reports. In the past, information referred mostly to internal data shown on scorecards, information that goes into KPIs. Big data analytics extends to the tsunami of external (crowd) data that is most often available in an unstructured format (such as text files, videos, blogs, and PDFs). Business intelligence providers have developed decentralized user self-service analytics applications that combine internal and external data for better decision-making. The analytics obtained from such programs extends from output that is simply descriptive to highly advanced artificial intelligence analytics and decisions proposed or made by machines.

Having in situ access to this kind of support will make Buyer 4.0 much more effective and enable far more informed decision-making.

We have already touched on the importance of analytics and the role it will play in making Buyer 4.0 real but it is worthwhile to look at it in more detail. Big data analytics is something you are likely to have heard of but you may not be fully aware of what it actually is. Big data in general embraces huge amounts of data that are too complex to be processed by traditional applications so that specific analytical tools are necessary to handle challenges that are mainly caused by the following[22]:

- Volume: Big data doesn't sample; it just observes and tracks what happens on a huge scale
- Variety: Big data draws from different types of data, such as text, images, audio, video
- Velocity: Big data is mostly available in real time as there are billions of touchpoints that stream data
- Veracity: Big data bears some uncertainty and is not fully trusted by many people[23]

It's also important to distinguish between the two broad types of big data, structured and unstructured.

Structured data (tables) is information displayed in titled columns and rows that can easily be ordered and processed by data mining tools. Think

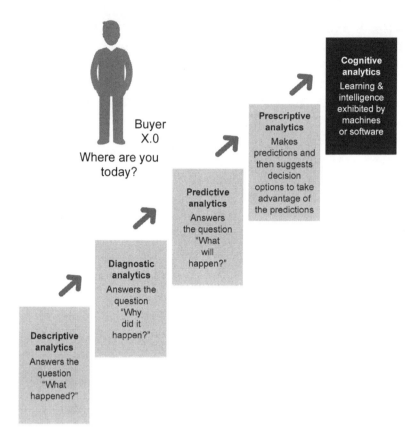

Different big data analytics

of a perfectly organized filing cabinet where everything is identified, labelled and easy to access.

Unstructured data (usually text) has no recognizable internal structure but is a mass conglomeration of random objects that are of little value until they can be identified and stored in an organized fashion. Examples include user recensions, Word documents, PDF files, spreadsheets, digital images, video and audio files.

The big data story in procurement hasn't been written yet but it inevitably will be just as it has in other industries. The modern era has brought with it a tidal wave of data that threatens to drown us all unless we learn to work with it. It is incredible to think that about 80 % of all data that exists today was generated in the last two years. To put that into perspective, consider this: Between the birth of the world and 2003, 5 exabytes (1018 bytes) of data were created. Some sources say, we now generate more than 2.5 exabytes each day.[24] That's more than 200 million e-mails, in excess of 50 hours of video uploaded to YouTube, over 250,000 tweets and well over 200,000 digital pictures created every minute of every day. To further highlight the challenges facing big data analytics tools, 90% of all data we produce is unstructured.

Looking at the maturity steps of big data analysis, procurement management has huge expectations. Currently analyses are often limited to show only spend transparency, something that's purely descriptive. But in the future this won't be enough if procurement as a business function is going to influence overall company competitiveness.

Processing transactional internal data is the reality in most companies today. Industry 4.0, the Internet of Things and sensor data are examples of source data that are starting to be considered in analytics and the same applies for unstructured data like text.

»Digitization of procurement is spot on what we are doing«

Interview with Jacob Gorm Larsen, Head of Digital Procurement at Maersk Group

Procurement 4.0 is still a fuzzy buzzword among other topics regarding digitization. What is the Maersk perspective on it?

There is indeed a lot of talk about the digital transformation of procurement with the entry of new technologies which will have a significant impact on the operating model for procurement. But this is still very much work in progress and a lot of the technologies are still fairly immature. At Maersk we are monitoring this transformation closely and also do pilots to explore how new technologies can help improve the overall procurement performance in our company.

Procurement at Maersk has gone through different phases in the past decades, mainly from being a transactional function to playing a more strategic role.

When more and more transactional tasks are done by tools and systems, what will procurement's value add be? What will make the difference?

For the future, I see three major differentiators that will change the procurement game: The importance of data as a strategic asset, the rise of cognitive and robotic solutions and the enhancement of the buying experience.

A prerequisite for digitization is to have sufficient data quality, which in fact is an ongoing challenge. In particular, how to structure data is crucial. Although we haven't found THE solution for this huge challenge yet, there are two things that make me optimistic in the long term: First, there is a growing understanding inside and outside procurement about the importance of good data quality. Second, there are new technical cognitive solutions that can help fix data quality. Solutions will come in pockets where we can make small improvement leaps. However nothing will be ready tomorrow, as this will be a long process.

As a differentiator, you mentioned cognitive and robotic solutions. Many companies offer software, apps, etc. Have you already made your choice as to which software, etc. you want to use to implement system-side changes?

We are starting to see initial use cases. Especially for supply chain management, a lot of transactional work can be done by tools. We are looking for solutions that can build a foundation for a diverse system landscape (with the aim of harmonizing these solutions), resulting in a »center of excellence«.

Of course, there are initial solutions on the market (e.g. IBM is developing Watson) that can support buyers in market analytics. But these are still small practical bits and pieces that support strategic work. However, it will have a bigger impact – I assume as soon as 18 months from now – on the transactional work sphere, where robotic solutions will replace head count on a certain scale. This paradigm shift will accelerate over the next few years.

Beside cognitive and robotics solutions – do you see any changes?

We expect significant improvement in enhancing the buying experience for buyers (and business partners). With regard to downstream processes (ordering), we will see an Amazon-like buying experience, which will move from B2C into the B2B world. With regard to upstream (strategic) procurement processes, we expect an »application« of the world, where a strategic buyer or CPO can access RFQs, contracts, KPIs and spend dashboards any time on mobile devices – easy access to real-time information and intelligence will be a must in the future.

All in all, we will see a paradigm shift affecting the operating model of procurement with a huge impact on interactions. Today many buyers spend time fixing operational issues. In a digital world these will be solved using highly automated transactional systems, and procurement professionals will focus on true partnership development and management. This is all part of the same megatrend.

Besides all tools and apps, there will still be people in procurement that work with these new solutions. How do you see their role in the future? And what implications will it have on the skill set of purchasers?

The digital profile will play an important part. On the one hand, a deep understanding of how a more digitized world and processes work is required. On the other hand, the ability to build high-quality relationships (with business partners and suppliers) is necessary. We will need more profiles with strong analytical skills and fewer with more traditional buyer skills.

Procurement is getting more and more control over people and spending, and at the same time has smaller and more specialized teams. Tactical and operational work will not disappear, but it will be automated so that procurement teams can focus on strategic work. The role of procurement will not get any smaller, but it will become easier to get the job done (and the »rest« will get back to business).

In reality, procurement more often than not operates within a defined spend cube because for some it's enough to have achieved spend transparency, or who buys what from whom. Considering the amount and nature of the data that is potentially available this is no longer enough. A whole lot more needs to be achieved within the next 5–10 years for any company that wants to be considered as a big data usage front-runner.

The obvious question is what should be the aim of big data analytics for procurement to improve innovation, supply security, quality and cost? There are two levers for harvesting existing internal and external data:

- Better decision-making by being better informed, having more transparency about costs and markets
- Leveraging information asymmetry in negotiations and before or during the preparation task, and being better informed of the consequences of offers in real time

In our opinion, there are two basic ways to organize the next level of analytics for procurement that need to be combined in an optimal mix of

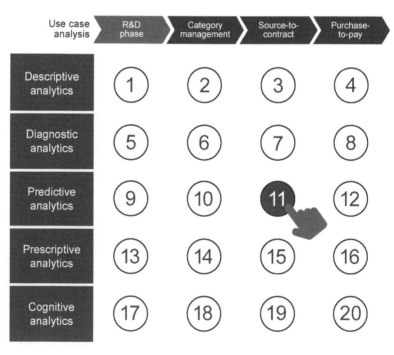

Analytics use cases

internal and external knowledge. Data analysts should do more than only provide reports like procurement controllers in the past. They should also be experts in analytics design for use cases coming from buyers.

- Adapted or extended roles (e.g. buyer, performance manager, cost analytics) creating new uses cases or being enabled for self-service analytics
- New roles: Data analysts/scientists in procurement

Descriptive analytics

1. Create an overview of *specifications, part numbers and standards* applied (same parts)
2. *Identify spend*, spend cube and tail spend/Identify *supply market characteristics over time* (capacities, prices, ...)
3. Leverage *digital profiling* of supplier representatives in negotiations
4. Identify *spend w/o P.O.*/assign spend solely in SAP FI to *category codes*

Diagnostic analytics

5. Identify *cost drivers*/Identify *similarities* in *specifications*/Enable *real-time cost calculation* (statistical models or bottom up)
6. Recognize *supplier performance patterns* (root causes)/Collect *price correlations* (specifications, load, cost drivers, ...)/Identify *cost impact of market price changes*
7. Assess financial and load situations as inputs for negotiations/Extract *»voices from market«* and internal audit reports about supplier performance/Optimize and *simulate the awarding mix*
8. Analyze *spend behavior* for *abnormalities* and optimization needs/ Analyze *material availability* and *disposition strategies*/Analyze *cash flow*

Predictive analytics

9. Identify *technologies & innovation suppliers*/IP, patent crawling/Predict *cost* and *price* of parts
10. Forecast supplier performance development, failure rates like ppm with external data (e.g. fluctuations, weather)/Calibrate bottom-up savings targets with external data (windfalls?)/Forecast *supplier performance, risks* and *insolvencies*/Forecast *market trends* (capacities, prices etc.)/Calculate *target prices* for the future

11. Predict *supplier load*, check supplier *capacities* with *internal AND external data*/Optimize *demand planning* with external AND IoT data (maintenance cycles)
12. Predict *future demand*, e.g. based on head count fluctuations, order intake MRO »consumption«/Predict *capability* of suppliers to *deliver in time, in quantity, in quality*, etc.

Prescriptive analytics

13. Propose *harmonized specifications* to achieve standardization/Identify *cost drivers* and show options to *reach target costs*/Map *applied technologies* with trends across industries
14. Recommend supplier *risk mitigation* actions/Suggest options to *design value chain network*/Capacity planning: Propose *optimized allocation of quantities* to suppliers
15. Show *carrots & sticks* as inputs to negotiate/Propose *negotiation strategies*/Get early *risk warnings*, affected parts and alternative sources
16. Optimize *disposition strategies* and *order points* based on supply market prediction and on demand prediction/Suggest *optimization of e-catalog portfolio* with external price data/benchmarks

Cognitive analytics

17. Calculate *optimized parts* dimensions based on overall portfolio (standardization)
18. Propose *future supplier portfolio* and *norm strategies* for procurement/ Identify *savings initiatives*/(cross-functional) *optimization levers*
19. Identify *negotiation patterns* per supplier and a*nticipate tactics/Fully automate negotiations (robotics)*
20. Enable automated (spot/best price) *ordering* & *»speculative shipping«*/Decide re-allocation of parts in case of incidents

It was revealed in the Procurement Leaders trend report 2016[25] that artificial intelligence is widely ignored by CPOs. However, CPOs are investing in self-service BI solutions because they have taken note of the case studies about predictive and mobile business intelligence.

Example: Risk management in purchasing

The world is an increasingly risky place. The combination of more people and businesses connected than ever before, geological factors, climate change and political upheaval represents highly complex and sometimes incalculable risks for purchasing in the management of global supply and value chains. Adding to the complexity are the internal organizational parameters, fragmented data structures, and entrenched paradigms that lead to non-transparency and diffi-cult-to-control risk management for purchasing.

However, the digitization of large quantities of data and various data sources along the entire value chain has resulted in new, early opportunities to iden-tify risks in the procurement process and the potential to create competitive advantages.

In the past, purchasing limited itself to collecting, evaluating, and then reacting to company, financial, and performance data such as the delivery reli-ability of suppliers. The information was prepared laboriously in stand-alone solutions.

Today, additional information, such as current geological and climate devel-opments, online raw materials development, country ratings from foreign offices, or ad hoc reports from the local press, is used and evaluated. This requires new types of analytical and technological tools in order to quantify risk information so it can be used to make concrete purchasing decisions.

In the future, intelligent, networked and independently learning computers will obtain, process, evaluate and visualize all kinds of risk information for purchas-ing and proactively make proposals for action. For example, if the production of an important supplier halts due to an earthquake, purchasing will immediately receive a forecast of current inventories in the supply chain, the time of produc-tion shutdown in the company's own plant, and lost revenues. But a self-learning system will immediately determine alternative supply sources based on existing specifications, calculate delivery quantities and times by considering available resources, and then propose an adjustment to the company's own production mix.

Maturity levels of risk management are described as follows:

Step 1 (predictive): Today, we are on the brink of having truly effective predic-tive risk management. Systems already exist that offer, for example, real-time tsunami warnings or the capacity to interpret political instability in countries where selected suppliers have relevant production sites. Yet few procurement organizations work with that data.

Step 2 (prescriptive): The next step needs to be a combination of external and internal data to create an early warning system for supply chains with automatically generated proposals for alternative suppliers based on current supplier ratings and other information. Those areas that are exposed, such as suppliers based in places potentially affected by tsunamis, are highlighted by push information to the relevant buyers. The buyers also get information about which alternative suppliers are available and what open capacities they have.

Step 3 (cognitive): In addition to Step 2, a cognitive system will automatically reallocate high-risk parts of the supply chain to other suppliers without any interaction from the buyer apart from perhaps pushing a button on a mobile device.

Social media could support these evolutions in two ways. Real-time filtering of information through microblogging sites or RSS feeds and specialized blogs could help to increase awareness. A good example here would be the environmental catastrophe in Japan in early 2011 and the nuclear escalation that followed. Leading automobile suppliers had to cope with massive disruption in their n-tier supply of electronic devices and most had very long reaction times after the news. Early warning and precise information could have helped a lot in reacting to such a crisis. There are more and more tools to support these preventive processes and activities.

Despite the obvious potential of big data it is not at present being widely used in procurement. Unfortunately, even the business intelligence providers generally just have supply chain examples available. For example, big data has been used to support demand planning and ordering, or on the sales side customer habits have been used to create sales strategies. In procurement, most mature big data analytics is used for the purpose of risk management. Packages such as IBM Watson and RiskMethods offer prestructured push information about preselected or indicated suppliers. Some providers combine human expertise and best-in-class technologies to offer tailored services rather than just offering automatically-generated data. Others offer pattern searches within unstructured data to identify failure patterns, failure reasons, categorization of failures, and predictive failure analytics. Everybody is keen to see how big data analytics can be used to make procurement more effective but looking at the current technology track it's clear that the journey has only just started.

Example: Supplier performance management

Today: Most companies have at least some supplier evaluation criteria that are more or less regularly applied to selected suppliers. Supplier evaluation results are stored in an audit-ready database and each lead buyer tracks improvement measures such as supplier feedback and development measures in a separate Excel template. The aim is to have a single point of truth without redundant evaluations from buyers worldwide in an unconsolidated approach. In the future, supplier master data must be cleaned and each supplier should have a valid worldwide creditor number. The future is exciting, but we have to take care of boring administrative work before we get there!

Future: When people shop online they make good use of the customer feedback that is available for all products. There are those people who read the five-star reviews to confirm that they are making the right buying decision, while others read the two-star reviews to get an understanding of a product's downsides.

For most companies involved in procurement today, supplier management doesn't offer such a differentiated evaluation and almost no qualitative assessment. Most suppliers hover around upper average performance of roughly 80%. Some are classified as preferred and strategic suppliers but we do not have the real insights from text-based ratings in online platforms and shops that allow us to judge a supplier's performance in detail.

There was a time when we used to allocate resources that enabled us to discuss the most appropriate evaluation criteria for suppliers. In the future, we will combine structured data gathered from the supplier evaluation process and combine it with unstructured data such as audit reports, voices from the market, press releases, and social media.

The benefit is obvious. Descriptive data is combined with diagnostic and even predictive data. It may be possible to predict expected performance losses in supplier fabrication by increasing quantities, for example. Today, a buyer needs to design complex and cumbersome evaluations and feed this table manually with data from different sources including quality reports and disposition data about quantity changes over time. Only after this laborious process is it possible to identify the corresponding quantity versus performance score and the maximum quantity that should be allocated to a supplier.

Furthermore, think about your most innovative suppliers. Are you interested in knowing which other customers they work with in your industry? The system would automatically check your strategic suppliers with regard to overlaps with competitors.

End-to-end: Efficiency boost

Efficiency will be another key quality of Buyer 4.0. Fortunately, increases in efficiency have been achieved in the last decade as a result of the automation of purchase-to-pay processes. We have seen such efficiency improvement use cases across all industries and even in medium-sized companies.

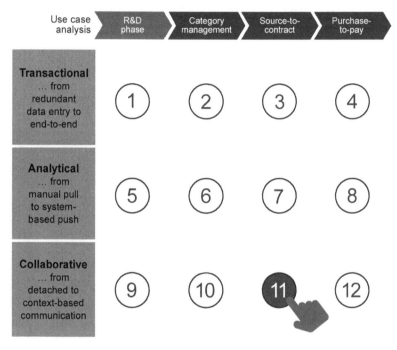

Efficiency-oriented use cases

Transactional efficiency: From redundant data entry to end to end

We understand the transactional process steps needed to build up the whole workflow. Seamless purchase-to-pay processes are nothing new. That's the area where most companies have already made significant investents in the last decade. So from our point of view, we see this as already existing necessity.

When speaking to buyers, most would say: »I have a dream ...«, that there is an end-to-end workflow starting with the sales or R&D phases with seamless process and data integration. At least there should be no paperwork, no workarounds, and no double data entries. A second dimension to consider end to end is a view on a part's or supplier's complete life cycle – not just snapshots rather a complete cycle from identification, ready for business, ready to order, development or phase-out.

Finally, we need to have intelligent systems that understand the current working environment. As an analogy, think about walking around New York with your smartphone. Your phone knows what's around the corner, what bars, cafes, restaurant, shops, museums or other points of interest you would encounter if you turned left of right. Procurement systems should also be able to offer informed insights into the effects of a particular awarding decision, which contracts need to be updated or which ones now conflict with the new contract, and so on. We do not have to blindly turn the corner and not know what to expect.

Use cases

1. Transfer aligned supplier list to Rfx/...
2. Provide approved supplier portfolio to R&D buyers/...
3. Provide supplier performance data/Transfer prices to P2P process and SCM function/Check existing contracts/Update contracts (life cycle)/...
4. Transfer of P.O. data to goods receipt and invoicing (incl. automated check)/...

Analytical efficiency: From manual pull to system-based push

Buyers suffer from highly manual analysis efforts during the category strategy process. Every analysis is done manually using information pulled from different sources. There's no push information and nothing digital, unless you consider today's standard process of web-search to be digital. All of e.g. Porter's five forces, which cover supply market trends, internal spend figures, external market volume expectations, material price changes, and trends in other consuming industries, need to be gathered manually. At best, there are some commercial databases available. All in all, it's still hard work to respond to the tidal wave of information, to make a category strategy work and gather all this data. In particular, push alerts about price increases and decreases can lead to a reduction of end-to-end exposure by real-time information about sales price changes on the clients' side and taken for price renegotiations on supplier side.

The key to success will be the move from pull to push data when buyers get relevant, pre-configured information about their category and their suppliers. Wouldn't this be nice?

Use cases

5. Find innovative suppliers/Identify & evaluate new suppliers (incl. risk)/Optimize costs together with R&D (cost value engineering)/...
6. Analyze spend and forecast demand/Identify technical trends & supply market opportunities/Track progress of category strategy implementation/...
7. Check supplier performance/Prepare negotiations/Optimize awarding (mix)/...
8. Benchmark prices/...

Collaborative efficiency: From detached to context-based communication and information

Are you proud of having implemented a web conference solution or a team cloud file storage platform? They're good starting points but collaboration will significantly improve by making it context-based and by enabling communication possibilities within a workflow.

Think of this scenario. You receive a drawing from R&D that has been uploaded to the awarding app and you have some questions about it. What would you do? What are your options? You could easily write an e-mail but this makes it difficult for you to explain to the R&D team which part of the drawing you're referring to. Clearly it would be better if all communication takes place within the workflow tool where all comments are documented in a thread. This is just a simple example of what could be.

Use cases

9. Align innovation suppliers with R&D/Align supplier list incl. new suppliers with R&D/...
10. Audit and qualify new suppliers together with SQM/Approve category strategy/...

11. Exchange Q&As with suppliers and internally/Align awarding decision with boards/Approve awarding decision/...
12. Approve P.O.s/...

»Time is money – we need to accelerate the speed of procurement processes«

Interview with Dr. Turan Sahin, Chief Procurement Officer at Allianz Managed Operations & Services SE

Digitization and Procurement 4.0 are on everyone's lips. How is procurement at Allianz affected by the ongoing changes?

Times have changed. Tenders for big IT projects used to run up to nine months, followed by another year of negotiations. While the total process took two years in earlier times, we now have to manage everything within six months. Digital projects are scheduled with 90–180 days before the final results have to be delivered. In this setting, you cannot have tenders with digital agencies that last months. You receive a request on Monday and by Friday you have a signed contract. That's how it works today!

To make this happen, manual processes in procurement (e.g. RFQs) need to be accelerated. Procurement has to be fast and agile, and still meet Allianz requirements in terms of transparency and compliance. Tendering processes at Allianz are usually tedious and requirements are complex. Start-up companies with less than 100 employees can't and won't do this. We recently placed an order with a company by the name of »the unbelievable machine« and we did so with fulfillment of all audit and compliance requirements as well as at a completely different speed.

Today, when you talk about digitization topics with suppliers, you don't meet with the Head of Sales but with the CEO dressed in jeans and a T-shirt. They are interested in lean and fast processes. Forgoing tenders is possible if the company offers something unique or something that does not yet exist in this form.

On the downside, we are confronted with giants such as Amazon and Google which have their own ideas on, for instance, the color of paper for contracts. Then it sometimes feels like two gorillas fighting against each other.

Are there any effects on the strategic work of procurement as well?

Strategic purchasers will no longer have six months' time to create category strategies. In the future, information will be provided online and it will be continuously updated so that real-time data is available at any time. In an ideal world, you get information at the touch of a button. Therefore you need a globally integrated data landscape. (Note: Alliance chose SAP Ariba as this supplier is well known and trusted, even though this might not be »best-of-breed« in all cases.) To make this venture successful, it needs to be transformed into an IT project.

At the moment, it takes us too much time to create a spend cube. When the end of a fiscal year is on December 31st and books are closed three weeks later, we still have to wait for eight weeks until figures are ready. And these figures were only 80 % accurate. It took us another six years to get where we wanted to be with regard to data quality. For the future, this data must be available instantly, with no additional effort required on the part of purchasing controlling, and business partners need mobile access to this data.

Sounds like looking in the rearview mirror to find out what is going on up ahead.

Yes, that's true. The weakness of our current tools is mostly the lack of artificial intelligence. People work exclusively with historical data, with no algorithms for anticipating future demand (Amazon is now further ahead). Category and supplier portfolios need to be structured properly by conducting ABC analyses and, as a result, they need to be treated differently. For »C parts« we see a kind of »Amazonization«, including, for example, guided buying with suggestions for customers (»Frequently Bought Together« or »Customers Who Bought This Item Also Bought«). This means a genuine revival of marketplaces, which will have to give up their proprietary positioning and let themselves be networked in any number of ways.

But tools are just one important piece of the puzzle. Analytical skills and industry know-how will become increasingly crucial, but it doesn't make sense to reserve capacities for this in the long run. Instead, they should be bought as required. Buyers need to become masterminds and »scout out« innovations from the supply markets. Entering close relationships with real strategic partners will be key for innovations.

We also see differences in how we buy – from product to service and from hardware to software all the way to software as a service (SaaS). The software spend will continue to grow and multiply, which will also cause increases in the IT spend. Because more services are bought than products, purchasers need to develop further and acquire new skills. The whole value chain in the insurance industry is changing. Procurement needs to take the role of value chain manager to converge the company's value chain with external value chains. Internal value creation and internal workload are decreasing, as can be seen in other industries, as the financial sector doesn't have the right capabilities and digital competence to handle related issues on its own. This also reflects the general trend of even more outsourcing and automation which, in turn, will strengthen the importance of procurement in the financial industry.

What will the focus of procurement in the financial industry be on then? In what way will procurement have to change on an organizational and personnel level?

The focus of procurement will change to product development, e.g. apps for customers that are based on a broad spectrum of bought-in services and competencies. One example: The customer and agent come in contact for the conclusion of contract and in the event of damage. We want to intensify this by means of new services and business models, e.g. no-claims vouchers or the possibility of workshop ratings as a trigger for incentives. This is based on external IT services, as well as product development and fulfillment, which don't yet exist in the company.

Today procurement is its own ecosystem, which will have to open up. For instance, the CIO wants to see the IBM spend on his iPad without having to call the CPO to get the information. The Digital Officer of Allianz has to ask himself the question of what the task of procurement is and how it should be organized. Is the current organization the right one? Do we need a digitization department in procurement or can it be interdivisional? At the moment, there is no clear picture yet. We are heading in the right direction with IT, but what about the rest?

On a personnel level, the development of diversity is very important. Currently procurement at Allianz has 23 nationalities that speak 35 languages and have different professional backgrounds. We want to improve this, especially by increasing the number of women on all management levels. To me, diversity also means cultural diversity, allocation and breadth of skills, functional experience through job rotation and external industry know-how.

Transform to a procurement app-oriented ecosystem along the core processes and a buyer's day

From a technology perspective, there has never been a better time than today. ERP providers offer new database technologies, simple interfaces to connect to an external cloud and internal databases, and highly experienced system integrators who can build a performant app platform for you. Furthermore, maximum benefits can be squeezed out of standard software because there are potentially huge external user groups whose instant feedback is harnessed to further improve new software releases. You won't gain a competitive advantage from individual software programming in standard workflows.

Buyer 4.0 will use an array of apps to help him with his work and he'll be fully connected to the cloud. Before getting to this point, there are some obstacles to overcome on the way to having a state-of-the-art, task-related and app-based IT landscape for procurement:

- Process integration: One end-to-end process with a high degree of automation
- Data integration: Fully integrated data within procurement systems and with other internal and external data sources

As was highlighted previously, buyers will benefit from customized apps on their devices. For example, just imagine a daily calendar or the timeline/roadmap to awarding major contracts. Several analytics steps, including collaboration over documents and others are necessary in preparation for a successful digital or face-to-face meeting. This is illustrated in the figure below, and shows how some of these applications can be used.

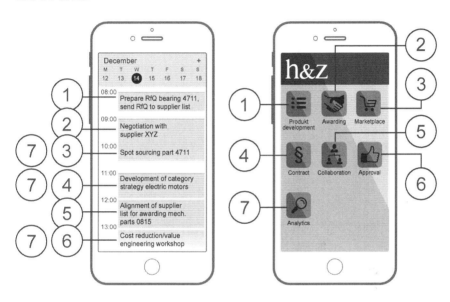

A day with Buyer 4.0

- *Product development*
  The greatest impact generated by procurement comes as a result of advanced purchasing or early involvement. Companies rarely have joint applications in R&D or in project businesses that involve parties starting with the sales phase. At the very least they might have stand-alone, individual software such as a sales funnel which is not connected to a demand planning category database and a project structure that does not perfectly match the category structure (two languages – project structure plan versus category perspective). In fact, mature solutions such as this don't yet exist especially when compared to other processes. Besides standard applications like milestone planning or project

management applications, such program or R&D phase applications tend to focus on collaboration.

- *Source-to-contract/awarding/Rfx*
There is a broad span of Rfx applications. From predominantly cloud-based SaaS solutions to highly co-innovated but still standard software workflow programs. The broad span of Rfx applications also includes basic workflows for simple indirect materials and direct c-materials, to complex workflows for indirect material orders. Changing to a modern source-to-contract solution requires, no surprise, some preparatory process harmonization. Many processes have become unnecessarily complex over the years but it is strongly recommended to challenge this trend. A basic Rfx process does not have to be complex. It can be kept lean and simple so the focus remains on the requirements that have the highest business impact.

Example: Old-fashioned Rfx versus future-ready Rfx

Old-fashioned Rfx

We seem to be efficient at using an application-driven Rfx process, but still upload Excel price templates to the platform. The platform is nothing more than a kind of e-mail application that sends out the attachment to the supplier. Automation is limited to an alert e-mail to the supplier to download the file from the platform. Suppliers fill out the template and upload it again.

And what do the buyers do next? They download it again, make an Excel price comparison, manually calculate a supplier comparison factor and maybe use other tools to simulate the optimal awarding mix depending on defined frame conditions. In the latter case, specific non-connected sourcing event applications generally need to be fed again with all the supplier data from the Rfx. Finally, buyers manually prepare sourcing board presentations and hand over supplier files to a contract management colleague, who then needs to key in data to feed their application again. That's a lot of work for little or no added value. Yes, of course, shared service centers might overcome such inefficiencies by employing low-cost labor but where is the real added value in this way of working?

With modern Rfx we are looking to maximize business impacts, but what are these impacts? Best practice today shows that Rfx documents are already using flexible price templates. Buyers can either choose the standard template (category-specific) or simply adapt the template depending on the requirements of the particular Rfx. Nothing new there, you might think.

But remember the tortuous process described earlier. It's not just the price template needed for the request, it's also the evaluation within the tool, applying complex simulation procedures (e.g. for transport contracts), and sharing results within the workflow with all participants from engineering, quality, and supply chain. All this has to happen before presentations such as the sourcing board decision paper can be automatically prepared and adapted for different target groups. By getting the sourcing decision approved within the tool, all the data is automatically handed over to the contracting party and system.

Excursion: Best-of-breed versus single (vendor) platform

What is a best-of-breed solution and what are the pros and cons of single platforms versus best-of-breed solutions?

Single vendor solutions

Most CPOs suffer in their work as a result of the fragmented IT landscape they have at their disposal. Some have not even been able to create a single sign-on function for their buyers, a situation which has led to high system changeover times, redundant data entries and different user interfaces. Some of these even have the usability and appearance of Microsoft's early versions of Windows. It's completely understandable for those struggling in such an environment to add a single vendor platform to their wish list. Full procurement suites covering all of the core and most of the supporting processes such as contract management are available. However, the degree to which these can be adapted to particular processes and functionalities differs significantly from one suite to the next, as discussed below.

Option 1: There are SaaS solutions with nice user interfaces and even iOS and Android apps available but, apart from some minor customization, it is almost impossible to adapt these. This can lead to major functional gaps between your specific requirements and what is offered through these off-the-shelf SaaS solutions, effectively ruling out their use.

Option 2: Then there are vendors offering custom development and co-innovation to merge your requirements with the product standard. The suitability of these depends on your fit-gap quota per focus process. There are other vendors providing real innovation steps in their software suites but to date there is no major reference case by which to judge how effective these can be.

Option 3: The third option is the do-it-yourself approach, or building your own application to match your needs. The major benefit is that you get a 100 % customized solution. On the down side, your company needs to be the innovation and development driver for that solution. You'd get no benefit from having a broad user group outside your company to give important feedback that enables updates and improvements to the platform as is typical for standard software.

Best of breed

So what about best-of-breed solutions? First, choosing a best-of-breed option and wanting to have a common user interface is contradictory. Best of breed involves choosing the best suitable solution for your functional requirements. In other words, one solution for contract management, one for awarding, one for spend management and so on.

If your major wish goes along with the same user experience (UX)/interface across all software modules, best of breed might not be your choice. Each software brings its own UX which leads to additional effort to create a common design. Developing such a user interface as a layer over the existing interfaces makes best of breed expensive. Actually, that runs contrary to the idea of best of breed.

In summary, best of breed might be a viable alternative to single vendor offerings in regard to off-the-shelf functionalities, but, so as to satisfy with your end-to-end targets, a data integration layer must, at the very least, be part of the design.

Chart list: Your top 10 apps today

1. *Standard BI analytics app:* Start with the app with the broadest spectrum of descriptive analytics, e.g. Tableau or Birst. It's your analytics foundation and base. Be able to creatively connect data sources, publish your KPIs quickly & easily with a self-service BI app. Define

new KPIs and use cases and get the full transparency about spend cubes, suppliers, the outside world and its impact on your procurement schedule to finally bring your KPI reporting to a next-generation level.

2. *(Supplier) collaboration & return on relationship:* An app, claiming return on relationship as value proposition, focusing on collaboration with your R&D, top suppliers in a particular market and including performance ratings, risk, and collaboration all in one SaaS solution. Such a solution serves as »digital information center«. With the help of new technologies, collaboration and communication among procurement, suppliers and business partners will be raised to the next level. The key phrase return on relationship will demonstrate that procurement has more to offer more than just savings.

Managing teams and maintaining the information flow is quite a challenge. Fortunately there are apps like Slack which offer you a platform or central point where all threads come together. The clue is the numerous possibilities for the integration of other services or apps (e.g. Dropbox, Google Drive, Trello, GoToMeeting and Twitter) so that you can cross-link all your useful tools. You can even integrate so-called bots which, for example, organize meetings for you. Communication via Slack is structured in channels in which there are only the relevant people, i.e. you can easily handle internal and external team members. This tool simplifies global collaboration, makes it much more flexible and can be seen as advancement of virtual meetings.

3. *Automated real-time cost analytics & target pricing:* Such an app goes far beyond traditional linear performance pricing. A statistical model identifies multi-cost drivers with regard to their significance. Usage examples include supplier portfolio optimization and cost reduction, design optimization in R&D based on a real-time calculation of alternative designs, and as a very special added extra it will determine the brand value of a company or product.

4. *Lever radar & cost out:* With an app called Bull's Eye, which is a 360-degree structured methodology to identify all the appropriate levers, evaluate optimization potential and define implementation meas-

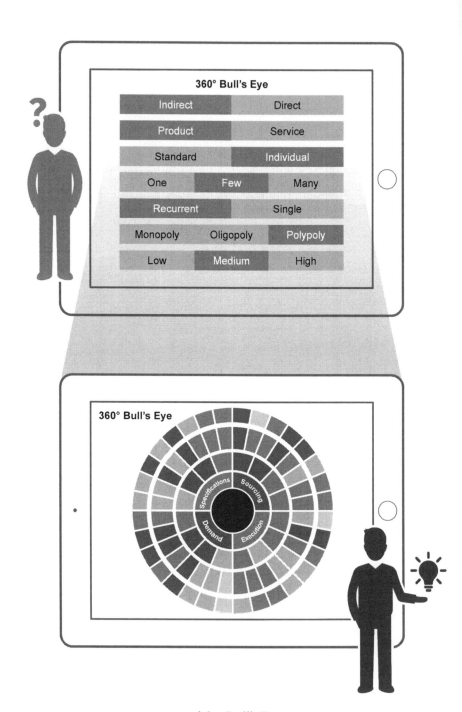

h&z Bull's Eye

ures, buyers can easily define their playground for cost optimization. More than 80 levers are described and stored together with practical examples. Using 10 key questions for an algorithm that runs in the background, the relevant levers are selected in a targeted manner and displayed on a heat map. An artificial intelligence extension might allow automated proposals for cost-out measures based on maturity level, history and externally-sourced big data about environmental opportunities.

5. *B2B global marketplaces:* Price transparency from search engines in B2C markets is much more widespread than it is in B2B markets. Today, frame contracts and corporate bundling are in vogue, but future marketplaces starting today go beyond the early 2000 marketplaces and need to become connected. Spot contracting in indirect categories instead of frame contracts based on global price transparency (price search engines) are seen as an opportunity for leveraging global price transparency and will easily reach tail spend in the future.

6. *Risk monitor & real-time alerts:* Based on the example seen earlier, this app starts with an alert function and also suggests recovery measures.

7. *Automated 3D cost calculation and geo cost comparison & optimization:* Automated cost calculations are based on specifications and CAD data for different regions and countries using external data or can be used to identify design outliers within a portfolio of similar parts. This gives answers to »what if« scenarios such as »what would we pay if we source from country X instead of country Y«.

8. *Performance & failure pattern recognition:* The identification of performance and failure patterns can be discovered from unstructured text data. Imagine using such an app to crawl through all your cross-functional supplier evaluation and audit reports to improve in the future.

9. *Automated negotiations and ordering:* Of course, there is demand quantity planning intelligence that considers seasonal data to optimize, for example, beer production during world soccer championships. Beyond such semi-manual analytics, today's apps are able to go through the whole process from influence factors, mathematical models, alignment with production capacities of suppliers, and terms and conditions and then plausibly check automated ordering. Even pilots for automated negotiations are available today.

10. *Digital profiling for advanced negotiations:* Digital profiling is not new and is already available as a service, especially for executive profiles. In the future, an app will automate data crawling for everybody just as search engines already broadly do today to find information about other people and anticipate their actions. For example, it could be used to get an online profile of a salesperson you will soon be negotiating with, including highly personal details such as their marital status, kids, interests, illnesses and so on. Such information could help prepare the buyer to anticipate which »game« the other might play and so could be particularly important for advanced negotiations strategies such as game theory, Chinese stratagems etc.

Is cloud technology a dream come true or a security nightmare?

Up to this point we have ignored one issue that has a huge, potentially devastating impact on digitization: Data security.

Cloud-based technology is everywhere. Its use reduces implementation times and increases employee mobility. Some big companies such as Amazon Web Services, Oracle, Microsoft (Azure), and SAP (HEC, Ariba) have invested significant resources in their cloud services. But many companies do not trust the cloud and still rely on in-house software solutions hosted on-site on an internal server on premise. For many, one of the issues of using cloud-based solutions is the fact that they are hosted by US American companies, which means the authorities there have the right to access the data. This is the reason why most companies force American software SaaS vendors to provide European-based cloud hosting at least. On the other hand, there's an upside to cloud technology in that it has significantly reduced entry barriers for fancy procurement solutions. With Rfx (source to contract) solutions alone, there are around 100 providers worldwide without a clear leader.

Think big: The ultimate scenario for digital transformation

First to mention: The e-catalog and spend transparency story should already have been written. Even thinking incrementally, changes must be taken to reduce your fragmented, disconnected IT landscape if you want to stay in the game. Usually procurement suffers from a fragmented legacy systems landscape fully packed with non-intuitive expert systems that are time-consuming and more documental than business-oriented. Many companies are facing a rather boring challenge to solve master data issues but it's one they must complete. This is bad news for all of us, even for ambitious CPOs, but master data is the key to unlocking the future. Some consider using external data cleansing services.

Cloud applications and SaaS increasingly offer fast solutions if only procurement could adjust the processes it currently uses to better and more effective market standards. Instead of multiyear custom development, a pure customization of software ensures fast (technical) implementation lead times. Such SaaS solutions are a nice way to digitize today's manual Rfx processes. In addition to such workflow systems, analytics apps can be tested in a stand-alone, scalable way. Doing it like this helps to avoid designing a white elephant as you can just try to identify the most promising pilots or pilot categories. How to go beyond this?

Procurement starts in predevelopment, and brings in the latest innovation from the supply market much earlier than any other competitors. Procurement knows the value chain, its dynamics, its pitfalls, its risks in real time. All non-value added tasks are automated up to artificial intelligence in non-strategic areas. Do you really want to negotiate office supplies or even advanced materials in 2035? Machine learning, fully transparent demand profiles and forecasts make it an easy job for procurement systems to perfectly allocate demand to best-price bidders.

Procurement benefits from perfect end-to-end workflows including all instant collaboration and communication activities within that context. Intuitive workflows make training obsolete, not depending of course on the generation using the system. Virtual reality training, hollow lenses and augmented reality support the buyer in all strategic, tactical and operational work and give stringent guidance like your navigation system in your car's head-up display.

Time is over for individual Excel-based price templates, differing from buyer to buyer, from awarding to awarding. The fully digitized awarding and Rfx workflow starts with standard costing templates and a template generator and gets an already aligned supplier list from the (pre) development phase. Importantly, consider new business models when suppliers are paid back to back based on pay-per-use models on the end customer side. For example, Audi makes plans for on demand or pay per use for some car extras like seat massage functions. These would be important considerations for your performance-based supplier contracting solution.

Analytics functions are fully integrated and offer buyers real-time simulation functionalities, cost drivers in supplier offers and outlier analysis. The perfect match and mixture of online and offline negotiations are recommended by prescriptive solutions for negotiation design. Like chess computers today, your analytics solutions recognize the sales guy's strategy and propose successful countermeasures and arguments. Finally, analytics is showing all relevant (big) data, supplier and salesperson profiles so that there is information asymmetry in favor of the buying organization.

And don't forget, buzzwords like joy of use, gamification and user experience are at the top of our agenda. We see user experience (UX) extending to three different areas. First, there will be different user interfaces for different apps but each will use the same standard icons, like Android apps versus iOS apps. Second, rising stars will have the same UI for all apps within procurement meaning that all apps have the same interface in the same way that Microsoft Office products do. Third, the interface will be the same but it will be customizable. For example, some people like to use fully packed websites while others prefer to have a clear structure. This same idea applies to how user experience is perceived. Some, but not all, companies think in terms of such a configurable IT landscape. In general, Amazonization provides the vision you should follow to facilitate a process that at its core is really something simple.

Design your way forward with regard to analytics. Change from manual pull information to push. Use highly qualified data analysts or data scientists in procurement to define differentiating analytics designs with the objective of getting the best information and recommendations out of the tsunami of information that we're at risk of drowning in. Buying analytics apps with provider IP algorithms is one thing. Designing your own to gain a competitive advantage could also be an option. Some procurement organizations with an eye on the future have started to employ their own app developers. And don't overlook the use of artificial intelligence. The full variety of analytics must be considered from the point of view of their potential business impact. Don't buy fancy software or technology just for the sake of having it.

Your survival kit

Change your procurement function to an agile, digitally-minded team and network ecosystem. Follow the agile idea of software development, including design thinking, and learn from the usage examples that came from early tangible software and apps, and of course prioritize according to the impacts you wish to see on your business.

No surprise – don't overlook leadership as the key to success in such a transformation – not all buyers have been waiting for digitization and the brave new world. A broad range of differing mind-sets from buyers at the age of 20 and buyers of the age of 60 must be expected and considered. And all of them are asking »what's in it for me?«

- Harmonize and clean-up your master data and fix process harmonization challenges
- Automate your standard reporting process and formats and free up resources for advanced analytics
- Check all procurement IT systems for their future readiness
- Rather don't invest in monolithic legacy structures
- Align your vision with regard to your roadmap with your CIO (state your needs)
- Start with promising stand-alone apps (be keen on agile and early tangible products)
- Discuss the uses of analytics with a view to gaining the maximum business impacts (be business driven, and don't follow a sprinkler strategy)
- Ensure the leadership of your company is fully committed to digitization and that there is the drive to push it through (even user experience needs digitization drivers)

PUSH THE BUTTON

It's all about a digital mindset in your head and in the heads of your team where you have to push the button. Digitization continues and will change much more than we ever thought of. This is not comparable with the age when IT was a so-called enabler. As you could see in the chapters, interviews and examples in this book, it's time to be curious, agile and courageous. You need to try new things and especially dare failure.

Take a closer look at where you are right now. Understand and calibrate your today's procurement organization, processes and IT landscape. Then develop a vision about your future operating model.

Regarding applications, no matter whether you are talking about analytics, market intelligence, or risk management, don't lean back and wait for THE application that does it all and has it all. Every single day, we are seeing new use cases and applications coming up. Yet we need to tell you that there is no jack of all trades device. Furthermore, some steps like the transition from descriptive to predictive analytics will probably require more than just implementing an application. Seize the opportunity of being an early mover, innovator or trendsetter. Start thinking like startups do!

And don't forget your organization and its individuals on that journey. Think about the spread of generations in your team and their individual digital frame of reference. Set up your own agenda to shape and develop Procurement 4.0!

ABBREVIATIONS

AI	Artificial Intelligence
B2B, B2C	Business-to-Business, Business-to-Consumer
BI	Business Intelligence
BPRM	Business Partner Relationship Management
CPM	Collaboration Project Management
CPO	Chief Procurement Officer
eCFT	Extended Cross-Functional Teams
IoT	Internet of Things
MRO	Maintenance, Repair and Overhaul
OEM	Original Equipment Manufacturer
PKAM	Procurement Key Account Management
SaaS	Software as a Service
SEI	Supplier-Enabled Innovation
TC	Technology Council
TPT	Technology and Procurement Team
UX	User Experience
VAO	Value Chain Analysis and Optimization

ABOUT THE AUTHORS

Dr. Alexander Batran is principal at h&z and head of the procurement practice. Dr. Batran has been in charge of procurement projects across several industries for over 10 years. He is also a lecturer at the University of St. Gallen. After his studies of technical business administration, Alexander Batran did his doctorate on »Supplier Development« at the University of the Bundeswehr in Munich, for which he received the »BME Science Award« in 2009.

Agnes Erben is a partner at h&z and manages projects for the professionalization of procurement organizations as well as the implementation of cost reduction programs. Ms. Erben started her professional career as a strategic purchaser for production material at MTU Aero Engines GmbH. There she got to know strategic, tactical and operational challenges as well as her passion for procurement. She graduated in business administration, inter alia with a focus on materials management. Additionally, she holds a Master degree in International Business and Law from the University of Sydney.

Ralf Schulz is a partner at h&z and is responsible for developing the consulting portfolio and products within the procurement practice. In addition, for more than two decades he has been supervising and managing projects in the field of procurement across various industries, ranging from strategies of procurement organizations, organizational design and development to strategic sourcing, innovation and technology management. After his studies of business administration and international law he gained comprehensive project and consulting experience in professional organizations, technology companies as well as multinational corporations and medium-sized businesses.

Franziska Sperl is a consultant at h&z and a member of the procurement practice and has worked on several global procurement projects, including strategic category management, reorganization of shared services, optimization of operative procurement and supplier management. She gained experience in industries such as shipping & transport, electronics, construction and financial services. Ms. Sperl graduated in business administration with a focus on management & leadership as well as marketing. As a part of Generation Y, she is especially interested in digitization topics, e.g. the tool-based automation of processes.

NOTES

1 Lambert, Douglas M., and Martha C. Cooper: *Issues in supply chain management*, Industrial marketing management 29.1, 2000: 65–83.

2 Darwin, Charles: *Darwin on Evolution: Words of Wisdom from the Father of Evolution*, Skyhorse Publishing, 2015.

3 Prahalad, Coimbatore K., and Venkat Ramaswamy: *Co-creation experiences: The next practice in value creation*, Journal of interactive marketing 18.3, 2004: 5–14.

4 Thiel, Christian: *Wer zu mir passt – Das Geheimnis der erfolgreichen Partnerwahl*, Humboldt Verlag, 2012.

5 Tylor, Edward Burnett: *Primitive culture: researches into the development of mythology, philosophy, religion, art, and custom*, Vol. 2. Murray, 1871.

6 Banerjee, Banny, Michael Barry, Pamela Hinds and Julie Stanford: *Project Innovation Through Design Thinking*, Stanford Center of Professional Development. 2016, Retrieved 21 November 2016, from http://scpd.stanford.edu/search/publicCourseSearchDetails.do?method=load&courseId=9165383.

7 Naiman, L.: *Design Thinking as a Strategy for Innovation*, Creativity at Work, 2016, Retrieved 21 November 2016, from http://www.creativityatwork.com/design-thinking-strategy-for-innovation/

8 Prahalad, Coimbatore K., and Venkat Ramaswamy: *Co-creation experiences: The next practice in value creation*, Journal of interactive marketing 18.3, 2004: 5–14.

9 Andreessen, M.: *Why Software Is Eating The World*, Wall Street Journal, 2016, Retrieved 21 November 2016, from http://www.wsj.com/articles/SB10001424053111903480904576512250915629460.

10 Saran, C.: *Satya Nadella: Every business will be a software business*, Computer Weekly, 2015, Retrieved 21 November 2016, from http://www.computerweekly.com/news/2240242478/Satya-Nadella-Every-business-will-be-a-software-business.

11 LEGO® SERIOUS PLAY®; for further information see: www.lego.com/en-us/seriousplay.

12 Lipman, Victor: *People Leave Managers, Not Companies,* Forbes, 2015, Retrieved 21 November 2016, from http://www.forbes.com/sites/victorlipman/2015/08/04/people-leave-managers-not-companies/#11b4a94316f3.

13 Pettigrew, I.: *Adam Kingl – The Generation Y CEO: The new breed of leader,* Kingfishercoaching.com, 2015, Retrieved 21 November 2016, from http://www.kingfishercoaching.com/the-generation-y-ceo-the-new-breed-of-leader/.

14 Meister, Jeanne C., and Karie Willyerd. *The 2020 workplace: How innovative companies attract, develop, and keep tomorrow's employees today.* Harper Collins, 2010.

15 Meister, Jeanne C., and Karie Willyerd. *The 2020 workplace: How innovative companies attract, develop, and keep tomorrow's employees today.* Harper Collins, 2010.

16 For further information see: www.holacracy.org.

17 Bernstein, Ethan, John Bunch, Niko Canner, and Michael Lee: *THE BIG IDEA Beyond the Holacracy HYPE.* HARVARD BUSINESS REVIEW 94.7–8, 2016: 38–49.

18 Denning, Steve: *Is Holacracy Succeding At Zappos?,* Forbes, 2015, Retrieved 21 November 2016, from http://www.forbes.com/sites/stevedenning/2015/05/23/is-holacracy-succeeding-at-zappos/#63d2a95840bb.

19 Fine Brothers Entertainment: *KIDS REACT TO WALKMANS (Portable Cassette Players),* YouTube, 2014, Retrieved 21 November 2016, from https://www.youtube.com/watch?v=Uk_vV-JRZ6E.

20 Webb, J: *Procurement IT systems and architecture,* Procurement Leaders™, Retrieved 21 November 2016, from http://www.procurementleaders.com/procurement-strategy-reports/procurement-strategy-reports/procurement-it-systems-and-architecture.

21 Thorp, J.: *Big Data Is Not the New Oil,* Harvard Business Review, 2012, Retrieved 21 November 2016, from https://hbr.org/2012/11/data-humans-and-the-new-oil.

22 Wikipedia: *Big Data,* Retrieved 22 November 2016, from https://en.wikipedia.org/wiki/Big_data#Definition

23 IBM Big Data & Analytics Hub: *The Four V's of Big Data,* http://www.ibmbigdatahub.com/infographic/four-vs-big-data.

24 Gunelius, S.: *The Data Explosion in 2014 Minute by Minute – Infographic,* ACI, 2014, Retrieved 21 November 2016, from http://aci.info/2014/07/12/the-data-explosion-in-2014-minute-by-minute-infographic/ & IBM: *What is big data?,* IBM, Retrieved 21 November 2016, from https://www-01.ibm.com/software/data/bigdata/what-is-big-data.html.

25 Procurement Leaders: *Trend Report Procurement,* Procurement Leaders, 2016.

INDEX

3D printing 15
Abrath, Andreas 7, 39
Active supplier 40, 46, 58, 67
Agility 12, 19, 40, 101, 110
Airbus 8, 62, 114 f.
Alert 37, 44, 148, 154, 159
Allianz 8, 149, 151 f.
Amazon 63, 75, 126, 129, 139, 149 f., 160
Amazonization 19, 150, 162
Andreessen, Marc 90
Apple 7, 17, 39, 42, 88, 100, 123, 126
Ariba 36, 40, 42, 150
Artificial intelligence (AI) 11, 15, 64, 74, 76, 112, 119, 122, 124, 133, 135, 142, 150, 157, 161 f.
Asimov, Isaac 122
Audi 18, 35, 55, 161
Austermann, Martin 7, 78
Automotive industry 17, 35, 52
Autonomous vehicles 17, 122

BASF 7, 39 ff.
Beckert, Armin 8, 114
Big data 15, 19, 21, 32, 40 f., 54, 60 f., 63, 74, 104, 112, 117, 119, 122, 127, 132, 135 ff., 140, 144, 157, 161
Blind spot 7, 25 ff., 118, 124
BMW 8, 18, 35, 111 f.
BP Europe SE 7, 32
BravoSolution 36
Business excellence 2

Business growth 27 f.
Business intelligence (BI) 36, 41, 127, 135, 142, 144, 156, 167
Business model 13, 17, 20, 25 f., 31, 41, 66, 76, 104, 123, 126, 151, 161
Business partner relationship management (BPRM) 40, 167
Buzzword 19, 27, 30, 32, 48, 66, 100, 104, 132, 137, 162

Cash benefit 12
Challenge 9, 11 f., 17, 19 f., 30, 41 ff., 61 ff., 67, 74, 76, 80, 84, 94 f., 99, 103, 106, 108, 110, 113 f., 126, 129, 134 f., 137 f., 154, 157, 160, 163, 169
Chief competitor 37
Chrysler 13
Clarke, Arthur C. 122
Climate change 11, 143
Cloud 8, 18 f., 32, 95, 121 ff.
Cloud robotics 15
Co-creation 20 f., 56, 64 f., 68 f., 71 f., 82 f., 86, 89 ff., 95, 97, 99, 108 f., 114
Collaboration 12, 14, , 18 ff., 32, 35, 44, , 47 ff., 54, 64, 67 f., 71 f., 75 ff., 89, 96 f., 111, 113 ff., 122, 124, 130 f., 133 f., 148, 153, 156 f., 161, 167
Collaboration project management (CPM) 85, 167
Commercial sector 11

Competition analysis 38
Competitive advantage 25, 27, 35 f., 43,
    50 ff., 66, 70, 90, 94, 104, 111, 143,
    152, 162
Competitiveness 18 ff., 27, 44, 73, 97,
    114, 137
Competitor 18, 20, 26, 31, 34, 37, 43 f.,
    51, 53, 63, 848, 94, 109, 146, 161
Conjoint analysis 37
Connected machines 15 f.
Connectivity 17, 19 f., 41, 63, 81, 87,
    115 f., 123, 128, 131 f., 134
Core competency 30, 43, 111
Corporate culture 2, 71
Cost competitiveness 44
Cost distribution 39
Cost leadership 27 f., 38, 64, 97
Cost optimization 26, 81, 157
Cost-cutting approach 29
Creative thinking 71, 92, 114
Customer market 26
Cyber-physical system 15, 71

Daimler 18
Darwin, Charles 64
Data 8, 12, 20 f., 26, 32 f., 36, 40 ff.,
    48, 54 f., 60 f., 63 f., 67, 71, 74, 76,
    105 ff., 112 ff., 117 ff., 122, 127,
    131 f., 134 ff., 140 ff., 150, 152 ff.,
    159, 161 f.
Data analytics 12, 19, 21, 41, 54, 113,
    117 f., 122, 127
Data privacy issue 76
Data security 42, 160
Data transparency 33
Design thinking 81, 88 f., 97, 100, 115,
    162
Deutsche Post DHL Group 8, 104
Differentiation 21, 25 ff., 34, 37 ff., 44,
    47, 65 f., 81, 88, 97
Differentiator 13, 44, 138
Digital gadget 20, 124
Digital native 123 f., 128 f.
Digital strategy 7, 74 f.
Digital technology 12 ff., 19, 106, 118
Digital world 118, 139

Digitalization 104 f., 114 ff.
Digitization 7 f., 17, 19, 25 f., 32 ff., 41,
    61, 64, 71, 74, 78, 99, 104, 106,
    112, 114, 116, 123, 126 f., 134,
    137 f., 143, 149, 152, 160, 163, 165,
    170
Disruptive change 32, 123
Disruptive system 110
Disruptive technology 17 f., 20, 89 f.,
    117, 122 f.

E.ON 63
Elementum 37
Enders, Tom 114
Enz, Robert 103
ERfx 21, 131
Extended enterprise model 13
External value creation 26, 43, 80

Facebook 88, 123
Ferrero 42 f.
Flextronic 12
Fukushima 20, 29, 37
Future scenario 22

Generation X 123
Generation Y 42, 106 f., 110, 127
Generation Z 124
Ghaim, John 66
Global trends 11
Google 15, 17, 88, 100, 123, 125 f.,
    132, 149, 157
Growth 11, 25 ff., 47, 54, 79

Hahne, Claus 8, 126
Hasselhoff, David 122, 124
Henkel 63
High performer 105
Hoke, Dirk 115
Holacracy 109 f., 113
Human capital 102, 107
Husqvarna Group 7, 78 ff.

IBM 138, 144, 151
Industrial revolution 15 ff., 114
Innovation 7, 14, 17, 19, 21, 26, 33 f.,

36, 39, 40, 43 f., 45, 49, 53 f., 65 ff.,
71 ff., 76, 78 ff., 82, 86 f., 89 ff., 95,
97, 99, 105, 111 f., 140 f., 148, 151,
155 f., 161, 169
Innovation capability 77
Innovation day 78, 81, 87 f.
Innovation management 67, 73, 105
Innovation manager 73, 105
Innovation potential 47, 54, 63, 70, 79,
96
Innovation process 41, 89, 96
Innovation project 56, 77, 97, 116
Innovation sourcing 33, 65 f., 89, 95
Innovation team 45, 96
Intellectual property (IP) 20, 38 f., 65,
70, 78, 88, 141, 162
Internet of things (IoT) 12, 15, 21, 60,
106, 116 f., 122, 124, 137, 167

Jespersen, Tommy 93
Johnson&Johnson 66

Kaizen 100
Keese, Christoph 88
Key account management (KAM) 81 ff.,
93, 97
Key differentiator 13
Key enabler 12, 14, 33 f.
Key managerial task 21
Key supplier 30, 33, 51, 77
Key technology 18, 25, 29 ff., 34, 36,
39, 43
Kingl, Adam 106
KK wind solutions A/S 92 ff.
Know-how analysis 39
Krause-Uhrmann, Matthias 7, 32

Larsen, Jacob Gorm 8, 137
Leadership challenge 8, 99 ff.
LEGO® Serious Play® 81, 91
Life cycle 20, 29, 57, 61, 80, 132, 147
LinkedIn 123
Linton, Tom 12
Lipman, Victor 103
Low performer 105
Lufthansa 7, 61 f., 64, 103

Maersk Group 8, 137
Mestral, Georges de 90
Microsoft 90, 155, 160, 162
Musk, Elon 11

Nadella, Satya 90
Netscape 90
Nießen, Michael 8, 104
N-tier 21, 30, 35, 37, 43 f.

OC Oerlikon Corporation AG 7, 74 f.
Organizational effectiveness 33
Organizational structure 43, 110
Original equipment manufacturer
(OEM) 18, 35 ff., 45, 52 f., 62, 87,
99, 167
OSRAM 35, 55 f., 60 f.

Papke, Thomas 7, 61
Porter, Michael E. 27, 147
Preferred supplier 46, 58
Price 14, 26 f., 33, 36, 40 ff., 49 f., 63 f.,
79, 100, 118, 128, 132 f., 141 f.,
147 f., 154 f., 159, 161
Price-oriented environment 27
Pro Idee 66
Process efficiency 20, 33
Procurement key account management
(PKAM) 81 f., 167
Procurement process 8, 14, 128, 139,
143, 149
Procurement system 18, 123, 128 f.,
131, 147, 152, 161
Product deployment analysis 39
Product management 19, 44, 85, 88
Product portfolio 26, 32
Profitability 26, 28, 90
Profitability 26, 28, 90
ProSiebenSat.1 Media AG 8, 126

Research & development (R&D) 14,
44, 47, 60, 65 f., 73, 78, 82 f., 85 f.,
88 ff., 140, 146 ff., 153, 156 f.
Rfx 18, 30, 121, 130, 132 ff., 147,
153 f., 160 f.
RiskMethods 37, 144

Rolls Royce 62
RSS feed 144

Sahin, Turan 8, 149
SAP 32, 40, 42, 64, 123, 129 f., 139,
    141, 150, 153, 160
Schiele, Holger 7, 49, 84
Scouting 45, 55, 67, 76, 78, 95, 108
Scrum 100
Shift 14 f., 17, 33, 38, 41, 55, 57, 60 f.,
    75, 77, 96 f., 102, 108, 138 f.
Siemens 63, 73, 93 f.
Siemens integrated control system
    (SICS) 93
Six Sigma 100
Smartphone 28 f., 107, 123 ff., 129 f.,
    133, 147
Social entrepreneurialism 11
Software as a service (SaaS) 125, 129,
    151, 153, 155, 157, 160 f., 167
Spend transparency 21, 40, 131, 137,
    140, 160
Stakeholder 34, 61, 74, 80, 82 f., 95,
    97, 103, 118 f.
Steam engine 15 f.
Strategic partner 46 f., 53 ff., 58 f., 64,
    87, 151
Strategy 7, 12, 30, 34, 43, 49, 53, 64,
    74 f., 92 ff., 111, 114 ff., 134, 147 f.,
    153, 161, 163
Success factors 33
Supplier classification matrix 58
Supplier cost reduction effort (score) 13
Supplier development 46 f., 54, 56, 58 f.,
    169
Supplier development matrix 58 f.
Supplier innovation 21, 52, 75, 77
Supplier interaction 7, 49, 60, 62, 77,
    84
Supplier management 40, 45, 47 f.,
    53 ff., 59 f., 64, 75, 79, 95 f., 145,
    170
Supplier network 20, 31, 34 f., 43, 111

Supplier performance management 145
Supplier quality management 47
Supplier rating 45 ff., 53, 144
Supplier satisfaction 7, 49 ff.
Supplier-enabled innovation (SEI) 14,
    66 f., 73, 76 ff., 84 ff., 89, 91 f., 95 f.,
    167
Supply base 9, 14, 20, 26, 53, 76, 87,
    118
Supply chain process 31, 37, 118
Supply market intelligence 76

Tesla 11
Tier 1 7, 18, 20 f., 25 ff., 29 ff., 33, 35,
    43 f., 75, 84, 124
Time-to-market 17, 21, 47, 65, 94 f.
Trust 55, 65, 70, 84, 92, 102, 108 f.,
    114, 135
Turkish Oltan Group 43

Unique business model 31
User experience (UX) 19, 76, 128,
    130 ff., 156, 162 f., 167
USP 31, 44, 105

Value add distribution 39
Value chain 9, 17, 19 ff., 25, 29 ff., 34 ff.,
    41 ff., 55 f., 62 f., 70, 74, 82, 93 f., 99,
    104, 118, 124, 142 f., 151, 161
Value chain analysis and optimization
    (VAO) 38, 167
Value chain designer 25, 30, 37, 44
Value chain management 42, 75
Vigneron, Jean-Pol 90
Volkswagen (VW) 18, 20

Walkman 124
Watson 138, 144
Weyandt, Jochen 7, 74
WhatsApp 64, 123
Wieland, Johann 8, 111
Win-win 62, 72, 111
Work-life flexibility 107 ff., 113